# Planning and Conducting Agency-Based Research

## Third Edition

Alex Westerfelt

Tracy J. Dietz
Texas Christian University

PEARSON

Boston   New York   San Francisco
Mexico City   Montreal   Toronto   London   Madrid   Munich   Paris
Hong Kong   Singapore   Tokyo   Cape Town   Sydney

## About the Authors

Alex Westerfelt has served as an evaluation coordinator for a community based health clinic and program evaluator for federal, state, and local agencies. He has taught undergraduate and graduate research courses. He can be reached at alexwesterfelt@sbcglobal.net.

Tracy J. Dietz is associate professor of social work at Texas Christian University where she teaches undergraduate research, field seminar, and social welfare policy. She can be reached at t.dietz@tcu.edu.

ISBN 0-205-38687-3

Printed in the United States of America

10 9 8 7 6 5 4 3 2 1    09 08 07 06 05 04

# CONTENTS

# INTRODUCTION

Historically, and up to the present day, social work educators have been aware that graduates of social work programs rarely *use* research findings in their practice and even less often *conduct* research in their practice (Epstein, 1987; Kirk, 1990; Kirk & Fisher, 1976; Marino, Green, & Young, 1998). In a survey of field instructors regarding assessment of their MSW students' skills in social work practice, field instructors rated understanding of research as the lowest skill area for students (Knight, 1993). In a survey of potential employers' views of the ideal undergraduate curriculum, agency personnel rated research as their least valued content area (Forte & Mathews, 1994). Yet the contexts in which social work practice occurs increasingly demand that social workers be proficient in evaluating intervention outcomes. Although course work in research methods is an essential component of social work education, students should also have opportunities to apply research knowledge and skills outside the classroom, ideally in their field placement (Dietz, Westerfelt, & Barton, 2004).

We developed this workbook in response to that challenge. Its purpose is to provide undergraduate and graduate social work faculty and students a systematic series of research assignments leading to a completed research study that students could carry out in their field placements. These assignments have three ultimate goals: (1) to increase students' interest and skills in practice research; (2) to help students produce agency-based research that contributes to the mission of the agency; and (3) to demonstrate to students the value and utility of practice-based research. Our premise is that once students experience success in carrying out a research project in a practice setting and see the usefulness of their findings, they will have the confidence and motivation to continue research efforts in their own postgraduate practice.

Social work has long recognized the importance of field education as a means for integrating knowledge and practice skills. We believe that the field setting also provides students an ideal opportunity to apply research concepts and methods learned in research courses and to see firsthand how their research projects can benefit clients and agencies. For a practitioner, conducting research in the field can lead to an understanding of the real importance that research results can have in daily practice.

## Agency-Based Research

This workbook is designed to aid BSW and MSW students in planning and conducting research projects based in an agency setting. We define agency-based research as applied research with the goal of producing information that can be used to improve conditions and services for clients. This is in contrast to basic research, which seeks to generate theory or lead to a deeper understanding of an issue (i.e., knowledge for the sake of knowledge). Agency-based research involves studying some aspect of the agency and its programs or its clients and their communities with an emphasis on the utility of that information. Applied research should inform action, enhance decision making, and lead to solutions of human and societal problems (Patton, 1990).

## New in this Edition

In this edition, we have expanded the chapter on Outcomes Evaluation to include material on the use of logic models and to help users develop program outcomes and the associate measures. We also provide additional information on using web-based sources when conducting a literature review. We have added specific chapters on Data Analysis for each of the types of studies, presenting more material on statistical tests and examples of ways to organize and present data. Based on feedback from our students and others, we believe the third edition of the workbook is even more user-friendly and will be a valuable tool in planning and conducting agency-based research.

## Acknowledgments

We would like to thank the following people for their suggestions for the third edition of the workbook: Rebecca Coleman, Grace College; Howard Karger, University of Houston; Jacquelyn Monroe, Ohio State University; and Wanda M. Spaid, Brigham Young University. We also thank our editor at Allyn & Bacon, Patricia Quinlin and her assistant Annemarie Kennedy. Jennette

Merwin copyedited our manuscript with fantastic skill. We received helpful comments on earlier versions of the workbook from: Ineke Way, University of Michigan; Arlene Kaplan Brown, Florida International University; Patricia Kolar, University of Pittsburgh; C.G. Kledaras, Campbell University; Tara V. Bankston, Louisiana State University; Cynthia Leonard Bishop, Meredith College; William Cloud, University of Denver; Nancie Palmer, Washburn University; Gregory Pettys, Washburn University; Steven Rose, Louisiana State University; James Stafford, University of Mississippi; and Barbara Key Wickell, University of Illinois at Chicago. We appreciate comments from participants who attended our workshop on agency-based research at the 1994 Baccalaureate Program Directors' Meetings in San Francisco, and from students who have used earlier drafts and editions of the workbook in planning and conducting their agency research projects. Finally, thanks go to Tom Barton for his helpful comments.

### Designing an Agency-Based Research Project:
# Layout of the Workbook

## *If you want to know . . .*

*What research the agency has already done?*
*What data does the agency routinely collect?*

*How do I develop a research question?*

*What has already been written about my topic and how do I find that information?*
*How do I write a literature review?*

*What is the best way to answer my research question?*

*How do I choose whom to study?*
*What sampling method should I use?*

*What procedures are necessary to safeguard research participants?*

*How do I analyze my findings and present my results?*

*How do I present my study?*

## *Turn to . . .*

**Chapter 1:**
Orientation to Agency Research

**Chapter 3:**
The Research Question

**Chapter 4:**
The Literature Review

**Chapter 5:**
Choosing Your Methodology

*See also:*
> **Chapter 6:** Survey Research
> **Chapter 7:** Qualitative Research
> **Chapter 8:** Single Subject Design
> **Chapter 9:** Outcomes Evaluation

**Chapter 10:**
Sample Design

**Chapters 2 and 11:**
Protection of Research Participants

**Chapter 12:** Data Analysis for Surveys and Outcomes Evaluation
**Chapter 13:** Data Analysis for Qualitative Research
**Chapter 14:** Data Analysis for Single-Subject Design Research

**Chapter 15:**
Writing the Final Report

# HOW TO USE THIS WORKBOOK

To use this workbook effectively, students should either have completed a research methods course or currently be enrolled in one. Although the workbook is designed to follow the basic steps of the research process as covered by any research methods text, it is not a research textbook and will not present foundation material. Rather, it asks the questions students must answer as they plan and conduct a research study. We intend that the workbook be used in conjunction with a research text, and throughout the workbook we remind students to draw upon their text.

The workbook provides guidelines for the development of four methods commonly used in agency-based research including survey research, qualitative research, single-subject design research, and program outcomes evaluation. For each method, we outline the steps we think necessary for completing a research study utilizing that method. We recognize that the steps laid out in this workbook may differ from those presented in other texts, but we expect that the differences will be slight. Further, we recognize that there are many acceptable ways of conducting research.

For each step of the research process we detail what students should cover when writing that section of the research paper. We recommend that students use the workbook pages to compile their beginning thoughts and ideas and then use word processing for more thoughtful first drafts which can be submitted to their instructors for feedback. These drafts can use the outline numbering of each workbook chapter for consistency and structure. The advantages of this option are to provide the instructor with typed copy, and once the instructor provides feedback, to allow students to incorporate it into their draft documents more easily. By the time the students have completed the workbook, they will have a substantial draft of their final paper.

Because the terms *field instructor, field supervisor,* and *field liaison* are often used interchangeably, we want to clarify the terms we use. In the workbook, *field instructor* is used to refer to the agency staff member who is responsible for supervising the student. *Course instructor* refers to the university faculty member who is teaching the course in which the workbook is being used. *Field liaisons* are typically university faculty members whose role is to coordinate the students' learning experiences in both the agency and the university. A program may give different responsibilities to different individuals; for example, a program may provide a significant role for a field liaison in the research project. When there are variations from the definitions or names given here, it would be helpful to designate for students the individuals who correspond to the course instructor and the field instructor as identified in the workbook.

## Special Note to Students

We recommend while using the workbook to guide your research project, you make a habit of referring to both your research text and the suggested article for the particular method of study you choose. In the Table of Contents you will see the four methods listed. At the beginning of each of the chapters we have indicated a specific article that will provide you with an example of a research study that utilizes that method. Reference to your methods text is intended for review of material; reference to the article will give you a complete picture of an actual study and examples of how to write sections of your own study.

Keep in mind that the research process is an ongoing feedback loop. As it is explained, it may appear quite linear, but in actuality, research activities may not follow the orderly steps we present. Inevitably, you will find yourself returning to prior steps to revise them based on what you have found in later steps. Eventually the pieces of the puzzle will all fit together. Trust us. We have designed the workbook in an easy-to-follow, step-by-step format that we believe demystifies the research process. We hope it will build your confidence in your ability to participate in and conduct research in an agency setting.

Even doctoral students whose research that is agency based will find this workbook helpful as they design their studies.

# Special Note to Course Instructors

The workbook can be used in a variety of courses. It is an obvious addition to a research course, but we intentionally designed it for use in a field seminar or a practice course that is taken concurrently with field activity. We encourage faculty to experiment with various options for coverage of this material. The following social work program components are considerations for determining the ideal format: research course requirements and expectations, block versus concurrent placements, the proximity of placements to each other, the primary instructor, and the other people involved in guiding the student project.

We include two suggested timelines for you in the Appendix: one for a 15-week, one semester course and the other for a 30-week, two semester course. These timelines are to help you structure the workbook chapters and assignments to best fit with the time available for your students' projects. A timeline for students to use as they progress through their projects is on page 72.

Some course instructors, faced with certain program constraints, may want students to complete only a research proposal and not actually carry out the project. Others may want students to work in groups and complete group research projects. In large programs where individual agencies may have several students in placement, students could work together on one project for the agency. One reviewer of an earlier edition whose program used a one semester block placement, told us that she asked her field instructors to develop research questions for their students. The students were given their research questions the first week and got started immediately on their projects.

A computer template is available to course instructors who adopt the workbook. The template includes the sections of the workbook assignments and may be used with your students. The purpose of the template is to enable students to more readily move their thoughts and ideas from the pages of the workbook to a computer. We hope that this aid will help students as they organize and write the first drafts of their papers. Once the first draft is on computer, revisions should be much easier for students. Further, course instructors may find typed drafts of the workbook assignments easier to read and evaluate. If you are interested in obtaining the template, you may contact Tracy Dietz at T.Dietz@tcu.edu.

## Special Note to Field Instructors

You are a key player in your students' research projects. Your view of research and the value you place on it will affect their experiences with agency research. However, you will not be totally responsible for helping them conduct the research project. The course instructor is responsible for teaching the students basic research methods and the application of these to agency settings.

Your role is to support and monitor the students along the way. You will be able to provide the best assistance if you are involved from the beginning. The steps we outline in the workbook promote your involvement by requiring students to ask questions of you and other agency staff. Your comments and feedback to them are necessary and will be extremely helpful.

You are an expert about your agency and its clients. You know what questions, if answered, will provide information that will benefit the clients. You may also be an expert in conducting research. However, you do not need a strong research background to work with students. If you lack confidence in your ability to help them with research projects, this workbook will serve as a resource to you as well.

Research resources for field instructors are available from faculty members. You could request that your school present a seminar for field instructors that focuses on conducting agency research. In addition, we provide a bibliography at the end of the workbook for more information on conducting agency-based research.

## Special Note to Agency Staff Conducting Research

This workbook can assist agency practitioners and researchers to fulfill their commitment to research. Whether developing an evaluation plan as part of a grant proposal or planning a research project, staff will find the workbook a invaluable step-by-step resource. For agency use, we recommend starting with Chapter 3 to clarify your research question and then continue with the rest of the workbook.

## A Final Note

We would like to hear about your experiences using the workbook. Your comments about what was most and least helpful will help us improve future editions. Please send your comments to us. Include the course for which the workbook was assigned and which sections of the workbook were unclear or difficult to complete. We look forward to hearing from you. Tracy J. Dietz, PhD, LMSW, TCU Department of Social Work, Texas Christian University, Box 298750, Fort Worth, Texas, 76129, or T.Dietz@tcu.edu.

# CHAPTER 1

# ORIENTATION TO AGENCY RESEARCH

Two major arguments support the need for incorporating a research perspective into one's practice. First, our professional code of ethics emphasizes the responsibility of social workers to understand, utilize, and conduct research. Accordingly, professional responsibility requires that we draw on and contribute to the knowledge base of social work.

Second, we are accountable to those we seek to assist. We are responsible for knowing the struggles, needs, and assets of those we assist and for providing the services that make a difference. Only through our continuous search for better understanding and the testing of current understanding can we effectively assist others.

As part of the curriculum in your social work program, you have been exposed to various aspects of research. Much of the information you have acquired is the result of others' research endeavors. In addition, you have either taken a specific research methods class or are currently enrolled in one. Now you are ready to move beyond the role of consumer of research to that of producer of research by conducting a research project at your field placement.

The best way to begin this process is by familiarizing yourself with the research efforts that have already been undertaken at your agency. To that end, we provide the following questions for you to consider as you begin your research project.

For students in social work field placements, start by talking with your field instructor and proceed to individuals he or she recommends. Often agency staff can help you understand the agency's own research program. You may need to ask more than one person to get a clear picture. Always be sure to indicate to whom you spoke and that person's position title.

If the agency has a research program, complete the questions in Part A. If the agency does not have a research program, complete the questions in Part B.

# (A) If the Agency Has a Research Program

(1)     What are its goals and purposes?

(2)     Who is responsible for overseeing agency research? Interview that person, and ask whether the research is done in-house or contracted out. If in-house, what is the size of the research budget? How many staff are involved in research activities? If done by contract, how often have studies been done in the past and by whom?

(3)    What resistance, if any, from staff and/or clients has been encountered in agency research efforts?

(4)    How and to whom does the agency distribute its research findings?

(5)   How have staff members used the findings?

(6)   What changes at the agency have resulted from research findings?

(7)    What is the agency process for obtaining permission to conduct a research study? (If there is no agency process in place, we encourage you to obtain written permission to carry out your study from the director of the agency. The procedures for study approval and protecting human subjects are discussed in Chapters 2 and 11.)

(8)    What studies or reports have been done at the agency? Obtain copies of two recent reports, indicate the purpose of each, and write a one- or two-sentence summary of each report.

| Report 1: | Report 2: |
|---|---|
|  |  |

**Now, go to section (C).**

## (B) If the Agency Does Not Have a Research Program

(1) Find out what information the agency collects for annual reports, funding reports, or community public relations. This may involve counts of people who use the agency's services, characteristics of service users, needs assessments, client satisfaction studies, etc. What information has the agency collected? If there have been no data collection efforts, explore why that is.

(2) How and by whom is the collected information used?

(3)    How and to whom does the agency distribute this information?
       How have staff used the information?

(4)    What changes at the agency have resulted from the information?

(5)    What is the agency process for obtaining permission to conduct a research study? (If there is no agency process in place, we encourage you to obtain written permission to carry out your study from the director of the agency. The procedures for study approval and protecting human subjects are discussed in Chapters 2 and 11.)

(6)    What reports have been done at the agency? Obtain copies of two recent reports, indicate the purpose of each, and write a one- or two-sentence summary of each report.

| Report 1: | Report 2: |
| --- | --- |
|  |  |

## (C) Staff Views and Usage of Research

Interview two staff members, one of whom should be your field instructor.

(1)    How do they view research? Write their responses here, indicating their names and position titles.

| Name: | Name: |
|---|---|
| Title: | Title: |

(2)    How do they use research to improve practice?

(3)   What research-oriented journals or books are frequently used by them? How often do they read these journals?

(4)   Ask each person how he or she has used information from a specific article in the past month.

## (D) Agency Resources for Your Research

What are the agency resources that will be available to you as you conduct your research project? Indicate below what you find out about staff assistance (clerical, computer, etc.), photocopying, mail, computer access, and anything else that may be relevant.

## (E) Timeframe for Your Research Project

Planning and conducting an agency-based research project can be overwhelming even for seasoned practitioners. It is a daunting task to complete a project as part of a one-semester course, so planning ahead is essential. We recommend that you take a few moments now and review the remainder of the workbook to see what lies ahead.

Pay special attention to the Timeline (page 72) for completing your project. A research project involves many, many steps and has multiple tasks to complete. Often your work will not progress in a step-wise fashion. You will be working on several steps at the same time and returning to work that you previously thought completed. We still believe in the importance of planning carefully and sticking to your plan as much as possible. Finally, allow time for delays and expect the unexpected. As Murphy supposedly once said, if something can go wrong, it will. We think Murphy was a social work researcher.

# CHAPTER 2

# PROTECTION OF RESEARCH PARTICIPANTS (PRELIMINARY)

We have included two chapters on the protection of research participants. We want you to consider safeguards for participants from the initial conception of your study through its completion. We find that students (and even seasoned researchers) are in a better position to prepare applications for review of participant safeguards and study procedures once they have designed their study. However, time constraints may require you to submit materials *before* the study is completely designed. Consequently, we introduce the process early on so that you can explore university and agency requirements. Then, in Chapter 11 we guide you through the basic requirements for protection of research participants.

Protection of the people who participate in a research study is a primary responsibility of the researcher. This obligation is generally fulfilled through the use of a consent form and through the early peer review of the researcher's study via submission of the proposed study to a review committee. These review committees are typically called Institutional Review Boards (IRBs), but some universities may have another name for their review committee. Agencies may or may not have research review committees as well. The responsibility of the IRB is to review all research involving "human subjects." We prefer the term *research participants* in keeping with our emphasis on the participation and contribution of clients in the research process. You cannot proceed with data collection until you have approval from the IRB.

Federal regulations provide the basis for IRB procedures and the actual evaluation of study safeguards, but the regulations leave room for varying interpretation. Thus, our discussion is necessarily general rather than specific, and the exercises that follow will direct you in learning more about your specific IRB.

An excellent on-line resource for more information about the protection of human subjects can be found at the National Institutes of Health's (NIH) Office of Human Subjects Research web page, http://www.nihtraining.com/ohsrsite/index.html.

NIH has also developed an on-line tutorial: "Human Participant Protections: Education for Research Teams," which can be used to fulfill the obligation for education in the area of human participant protection, http://cme.cancer.gov/c01/. The course presents information related to protection of human participants, and includes text, case studies, and exercises to help researchers learn the basics of human subjects protection.

You must submit your study design for review *before* you begin collecting data. Some IRBs have strict time frames for review of and response to submissions. As noted above, this may necessitate a submission from you *before* you have had time to complete the necessary sections of this workbook and develop your study design. In that case, you need to work closely with your course instructor to meet the IRB requirements.

Keep in mind that it is *not* the function of these committees to evaluate your study design and methods, but rather to evaluate the extent to which you will protect research participants from any harm. This includes physical, social, psychological, and legal harm.

For example, if you are studying people recently paroled from prison, how will you make sure they do not feel any coercion to participate in your study? What if they mistakenly believe that their parole officer *expects* them to participate? For some studies you must address how you will handle information you receive that involves illegal behaviors. You will always have to discuss how you will keep information confidential.

Consider what is needed if your study involves sensitive information. For example, if you ask information about a past sexual assault and a person becomes emotionally upset, what are your plans to handle that type of situation? As part of your application for IRB approval, you must describe all potential risks involved in your study and the procedures for protecting against or minimizing those risks, including risks to confidentiality.

## Reminder:
Build enough time into your study's timetable
to allow the IRB to review your application.

## (A) The University IRB

Students conducting research projects as part of their educational requirements must submit an application for human subjects protections with their university IRB. Find out the name of the university IRB and contact its chairperson regarding application for approval of your study's procedures. Obtain a copy of the application packet to review and begin preparing. Be sure to ask about the time frames for submission of applications and the expected date for response.

Indicate below with whom you talked and what information you received.

## (B) The Agency IRB

Find out the agency's procedure for the review and approval of research studies. Ask for a copy of the procedures for submission. Also ask about the time frames for submission of applications and the expected date for response.

If the agency has no formalized procedures, we strongly encourage you to submit to the agency your University IRB application, and obtain, in writing, the agency director's permission to carry out your study.

Indicate the names of those with whom you talked and what information you received.

## (C) Prepare a Timeline for Your Human Subjects' Review Application

If you need to submit your application for approval of study procedures very soon, consult the IRB guidelines and turn to Chapter 11 to prepare your application.

| TASKS | DATES |
|---|---|
| First draft of IRB application due to your course instructor<br>*Receive comments from your course instructor and make corrections based on instructor feedback.* | _____ |
| First IRB application due to University IRB committee* | _____ |
| Agency application due | _____ |
| First IRB notification on your application expected*<br>*Once application is approved, data collection can begin. Keep in mind that you may have to make revisions and resubmit.* | _____ |
| If applicable, resubmission due | _____ |
| If applicable, final IRB approval expected | _____ |

*After course instructor approval, add the starred dates to your study timeline on page 72.

# CHAPTER 3

# THE RESEARCH QUESTION

**Reminder:**
Review the section of your research text regarding formation of the research question, problem, or topic.

In this chapter you will develop your initial research question. We say "initial" because oftentimes as people begin looking at articles related to their topic of interest, they learn more about the topic or about ways it has been studied that help them reshape their research question. We want to help you to brainstorm possible questions of interest to you. Developing a clear research question is crucial to help you stay focused as you complete the other steps of the study. *We encourage students,* once they have finalized their research questions, to write it inside the cover of the workbook or somewhere prominent in their notebooks or study folders. Referring to it as you review the literature will help you avoid feeling overwhelmed or from going off on a tangent.

Keep in mind that a research question is not the same as a hypothesis. A hypothesis is your expectation about how events or phenomena will be related *based on some prior study and understanding of the events or phenomena.* A research question is just that, a question. It asks exactly what you would like to know, *not* what is already known or what can be expected. For example, "What is the impact of chronic illness on children's coping skills?" is a research question. A hypothesis is a statement. "Children living with chronic illness will have fewer coping skills than children who are not chronically ill" is an hypothesis.

Social workers assess client strengths and successes as readily as they assess problems and needs. As you think about possible questions for your study, consider research questions that seek to learn not only about problems and needs, but also about strengths and successes. We encourage this approach in research.

Discovering how people survive stressful situations and crises contributes valuable information to the profession as it develops programs and services. Uncovering the strengths of certain types of families or communities can enhance workers' practice knowledge. Allowing people to tell their stories in their own words not only recognizes that they have much to offer but also reminds us that research, like practice, can benefit from a cooperative, interactive approach. We strongly encourage you to be as interested in "what is going right" as in "what is going wrong." Answering each of the following questions will guide you in developing your research question. As ideas come to mind, put them in question form.

# (A) What Would You Like to Know?

Perhaps you are interested in knowing more *about the clients* who are served by the agency:
   —their characteristics
   —their strengths and assets
   —their specific needs
   —their satisfaction with the agency's services
   —the obstacles they face, either in daily living
      or in accessing services
   —how they are affected by agency services
      or lack of agency services

Perhaps you are interested in knowing more *about the services* at your agency:
   —the extent to which services address the needs
      of people in the community
   —their success in reaching the target population
   —their impact or effectiveness (outcomes)

Perhaps you are interested in knowing more *about the workers* at the agency:
   —their practice orientation
   —their job satisfaction

Write your initial ideas for a research topic here.

# (B)  What Would the Agency Like to Know?

(1)    Talk to your field instructor or anyone else at the agency she or
       he recommends as a good source of information for this
       question. Jot down their ideas for research they think would be
       of value to the agency. Be open to all their ideas and begin
       thinking of possible research questions that might blend their
       interests with yours.

       Indicate the names of people to whom you spoke and their
       position in the agency. What topics are they interested in? Put
       their ideas into questions.

| Name: | Interest: |
|-------|-----------|
|       |           |

(2)    Present your ideas to them for your research question. Indicate
       their feedback below.

| Name: | Feedback: |
|-------|-----------|
|       |           |

## (C) What Would the Clients Like to Know?

Check with your field instructor about talking to some of the clients with whom you have contact. If you don't yet have contact, ask your field instructor to recommend to you some clients with whom you could talk about this.

Our students' experiences have been that using the word "research" can be as confusing to clients as to students. So, we recommend that you avoid using the word "research" when talking with them. Rather, tell clients that, as a student, you are interested in gathering information that would be helpful to the agency. Ask them what topics they think might be helpful for the agency to know more about.

Indicate the first names or initials of people to whom you spoke. What topics would they be interested in learning more about? Put their ideas into questions.

| Name/Initials: | Ideas: |
|---|---|
| | |

## (D) What Is Your Research Question?

Now take your first stab at coming up with a research question. Based on your thinking, interests, and discussions with others, write out one or two questions you would be interested in pursuing.

Following, we provide some research questions that our students have studied, organized by the type of study they designed.

# List of Student Research Questions and Design Type

## Survey Research
- What Is the Employee Turnover and Job Satisfaction in the Field of Disabilities?
- What Is Foster Parent Satisfaction of Case Management Services Provided by Private Versus Public Agencies?
- How Does Attitudinal Change Relate to Length of Stay for Substance Abusers in Treatment?
- What Are the Characteristics of Programs in Public Administration Offices for Court-Appointed Guardians?
- What Are the Characteristics of Juvenile Offender Recidivists?
- What Are the Needs of Jewish Elders?

## Qualitative Research
- How Do Nurse Case Managers and Social Worker Case Managers Describe Case Management Roles?
- What Are the Ethical Restrictions on Dual Relationships among Different Mental Health Professions?
- What Are the Factors Leading to Relapse in Women Who Are Chemically Addicted?
- What Are the Experiences of Clients with Severe and Persistent Mental Illness Who Are in Community Corrections?

## Single-Subject Design
- What Is the Effect of Classroom Reinforcement on Classroom Behavior Change?
- What Is the Effect of Physical Exercise on an Alzheimer's Patient's Aggressive Behavior to Others?

## Outcomes Evaluation
- How Does Staff Training Improve Staff Knowledge about Sexuality for People with Disabilities?
- How Effective Is a Cultural Consciousness-Raising Group on Empowerment of Latino Women?
- How Effective Is an Anger Management Group on Skill Development of Sixth Graders?
- How Effective Is an Educational Support Group for Hepatitis C Patients?

## (E)  Browse the Literature Related to Your Topic

Now make a quick trip to the library or search an on-line database just to see what information is available on your topic. This is *not* the time to do a thorough literature review; that will come later. For now, simply see if there are several current articles on your topic and choose two (preferably from social work journals). Don't hesitate to ask reference librarians for help.

Skimming over these articles will give you an idea of the scope of the topic you have chosen and may help you in narrowing down your question. Our experience is that many students significantly change their question based on this first view of the literature. If, in the middle of this step—or the next one—you become less than enthusiastic about your research question, do not hesitate to abandon it and pursue another.

For now, list the author, title, and reference information for two articles you examined and a two- or three-sentence summary of each.

(1)    Author and Date:

       Title:

       Citation Information:

       Summary:

(2)    Author and Date:

       Title:

       Citation Information:

       Summary:

# (F)  Refine Your Research Question

Refine your research question based on your literature review using the following checklist:

✓ Is the research question relevant to social work? How does the issue involve social work?

✓ What makes this issue or problem significant? What is the scope of the issue? (Who is affected? How many people are affected? In what ways?)

✓ By answering your question, how could the information impact services to clients at your agency or improve practice?

✓ Is a study to answer your question feasible? In other words, can you reasonably do what is necessary to answer your research question? Address this relative to the time you have been given to do the study, money that is available for expenses of the study (e.g., photocopying, mailing, etc.), ethical and logistical considerations, the amount of assistance you will need from others (interviewers, computer consultation, practice consultation, data analysis, etc.), and the amount of cooperation you will need from agency personnel. Be realistic in your estimations because it may help you focus a research question that is too ambitious.

✓ Which research method will you use? Finally, begin to think about the best way (research method) to answer your question. Would qualitative or quantitative methods be most appropriate? (Don't hesitate to return to your methods text for a quick review of these approaches.) This workbook offers guidance on four methods of research: survey, qualitative, single-subject design, and outcomes evaluation. Which method do you think would provide the best information to answer your question? Why?

## (G) Finalize Your Research Question

Share your research question with your peers and field instructor, soliciting their feedback.

Indicate below the names of people you asked for feedback and what questions or suggestions they had.

| Name: | Feedback: |
| --- | --- |
|  |  |

Write your research question below:

# CHAPTER 4

# THE LITERATURE REVIEW

One of the main purposes of conducting a literature review is to help you become more knowledgeable about your research topic. Keep in mind that a literature review is both a process and a product. The process of conducting a literature review helps you learn more about your topic and provides guidance on how to carry out your own study. You will conduct a better study if you know what other people have said about your topic, what they have found in their own studies, and how they designed their studies. The product of conducting a literature review is a written review that explains the importance and relevance of your topic based on what has already been written and shows how your study will add to what is already known.

*Quantitative* methods typically involve a deductive approach to research. Thus, you begin by reviewing the literature to develop your ideas regarding what information to collect in your study. In *qualitative* research, there is a debate about when to review the literature. Some proponents of qualitative research suggest doing the literature review later in the study. According to this view, your research will be "pure" in the sense that it will not be guided or biased—perhaps in a wrong direction—by what is known about your topic and what has been done by other researchers. Other qualitative researchers value the early review of literature to better understand the topic and to design the best possible study.

We believe that reviewing the literature first is essential, and we guide you in completing that step before you proceed with the other steps of conducting either a quantitative or qualitative study. This way you can compare your plans for your study to what others have done with an eye for improving your project. A literature review can keep you from "reinventing the wheel" by suggesting ways to conceptualize (define) the question and operationalize (measure) the variables. The literature will also help you identify existing measurement instruments. While a considerable part of the literature review is conducted early, remember to think of the literature review as an ongoing process. As your project unfolds and new questions arise, you will return to the literature for answers.

We assume you have access to a college library or the internet and computerized databases of abstracts and indexes relevant to social work, and that you are able (or will learn) to use them. Before sitting down at the keyboard, review and write down your research question. As you examine articles, keep your question in front of yourself to stay focused. This is a simple step that will help you stay on track.

Electronic searching is powerful and fast, but you can easily overdo it by locating literature that is, at best, peripheral to your topic. Before you start to search the literature, learn how to search effectively, how to do an advanced search, and how to expand or narrow your search, using Boolean operators, truncated terms or wildcards, and other features of electronic databases. Reference librarians are a tremendous help and we strongly urge you to work with librarians at your library.

We recommend that you keep a log of where and how you have searched the literature (see pages 42-45). If you later need assistance from a reference librarian or your instructor, you will be able to show them what you have already tried. The process of recording what you have done will also help you learn effective searching strategies.

Given the increasing availability of web-based information, it is critical to carefully evaluate the sources you will use in your study. In general, published literature (articles in professional journals) has undergone a peer review process in which manuscripts are reviewed by authorities in that area of research before being accepted for publication. This is not the case for web-based sources. Web sources can provide factual information, promote opinions or viewpoints, or present inaccurate information.

Many university libraries provide guidelines or criteria for evaluating web-based sources. At a minimum, you should consider:

- Who is the author? What are his or her qualifications and credentials? Is this person a reputable source on the topic?

- Is the information accurate? Are references and links to related sites given? If the site does not present primary data, from where did the information come? Is the original source cited? In general, use actual research studies, not reports about a study that can misrepresent the author's intended meaning. Watch for errors in web sources. Grammatical and typographical errors should lead you to question the validity of the information on the site.

- Is the information current? What is the date on the site? When was it last revised?

- Is the information objective? Who sponsors the site? Avoid sources that offer opinions, attempt to persuade you, or sell products.

- Does the source provide comprehensive information? Is there depth and detail as well as breadth about the topic? Are reputable links given?

Evaluate all literature, including that published in quality journals, for its reliability, validity, and limitations. All studies have limitations and they are usually presented and discussed by the authors. Assess the impact of the limitations on the study's findings. These are ways you become a critical reader of research literature.

## Helpful Tips:

✓ Students often have difficulty determining whether an article is empirical or not. An empirical article is based on observations and reports the results of an actual study that was designed and completed by the authors. *These will be your most valuable resources when designing your study.* The authors provide information about the people who were in their sample, how the data were collected, and the findings. With few exceptions, the article will contain tables of data or, in the case of qualitative studies, excerpts from participant interviews. We recommend that you locate at least four articles about original research studies that present as much information as possible about the design and execution of the study. They will provide examples to assist you in designing your study.

✓ Some articles will report findings from other studies. These are not empirical articles as they usually do not contain information about how the study was conducted. However, the articles will include the source of the empirical articles they are citing.

✓ "I can't find anything on my topic. There have been no studies done on this at all." This is the most common difficulty reported by students doing a literature review. Yes, often students cannot find anything; but it is seldom true that no work has been done on the topic. What we frequently find is that either the student has not sought the assistance of reference librarians who can help tailor a search of the literature, or the student is too narrowly restricting the search. For example, if the research question is to determine the needs of a community of First Nations people for their local service center, there may be no other published needs assessment of that group. However, you can probably find published studies of the needs of First Nations people in general—for example, surveys regularly conducted by the Indian Health Service. Also, you can locate articles that detail needs assessments done among other ethnic groups. Such articles, while not addressing your target group, will provide you with information on how to conduct a needs assessment with an identified group of individuals.

✓ Don't just use abstracts. Abstracts are brief summaries that should help you determine the relevance of the article to your work, but should not be used as a main source. If you must use abstracts because you are unable to access the full article, note that the information you are citing comes from the abstract.

✓ We encourage students to focus their efforts on identifying articles rather than books because articles are easier to digest. One exception is an edited book that often contains, in essence, a series of articles on a particular topic. Books that are complete reports of a single study or a series of studies can also be helpful. Dissertations completed by persons outside your own university can be difficult to obtain in a timely fashion. (They are sometimes identified in search results simply with the designation, Ph.D. or D.S.W.)

✓ You will find one of the best sources for references at the end of each article. All articles and books will list their references, and once you have identified a relevant work, its bibliography will provide you with several other sources of material. This is why finding the most recent literature is important. Authors are able to cite only works prior to their own.

✓ Keep in mind the overall purpose of conducting a literature review as you browse the literature. You should be looking for articles that:

- Introduce and provide a background for your topic
- Establish the importance of your topic
- Provide a theoretical basis for your study
- Address a client issue similar to yours
- Identify and operationalize variables used in prior studies
- Identify measurement instruments and methods of study
- Present findings on your topic
- Highlight an intervention or program similar to yours
- Address issues about your population

✓ *A word of warning.* Too often students have spent many hours, even days, in the library and come to us in frustration because they have nothing to show for their efforts. Do not make the same mistake. Start your search early and regularly seek help. Consult with your librarians and instructors frequently. Remember: *Seek assistance at the first sign that you are not getting anywhere.*

You should include a minimum of 10 references, no less than four empirical articles (actual studies with sample, methods, and findings), and at least six other scholarly references. The dates of publication of articles should be within the past five years. There are some exceptions to this—for example, a "classic" work that was written many years ago. Also, in a few cases you may find that your topic has rarely been studied and requires a search beyond the past five years.

## Reminder:

Be sure that you know how to conduct a literature search using electronic databases on-line or in the library. Do not simply do a search on the Internet. Ask reference librarians for assistance. They can save you much time.

# (A) Conduct a Literature Search

The following directions will guide you step-by-step through the process of locating literature relevant to your research question. Remember to record what you have done and where you have looked.

(1)     Ask your course instructor if he/she can recommend any faculty members who are knowledgeable about the topic of your study or population of interest. Talk to suggested faculty members, your field instructor, and other people at your agency to obtain their recommendations for references. Sometimes, locating the right person can give you the bulk of your references.

Indicate with whom you talked, when, and the results.

(2)    Begin searching the literature by choosing key search words.

List them here (ask your professor and/or librarian for their advice):

(3)    List here the databases you will use for your search. Obtain information on how to access them, if you do not know already. We recommend *Research Navigator Guide: The Helping Professions* (2004), for help with your literature search.

(4)   Go to your first database and begin entering the requested information.

   (a)   Set the computer search so that it returns the abstract for each reference. This will help you to do the initial gleaning of the list.

   (b)   Limit your search to the last five years to start. If that does not generate enough references, do not be too quick to go back more years. Rather, reconsider your search words.

   (c)   If you use the PsychLit abstracts, in the P.T. field (publication type) you can specify empirical study and it will limit the search to return empirical studies only.

(5)   Search!

   If the search results include significantly more than about 40 or 50 references, you will need to further narrow your search words or dates so that you have a manageable list of references to review. Do not hesitate to get assistance with this task.

(6)   Once you have a successful search list, read through it several times.

   (a)   Read the abstracts in the list and highlight references that appear to be on target with your question.

   (b)   Highlight any article that is titled "A Review of the Literature." It will provide an overview of the literature related to your topic and can save you much time.

(7)    Submit the results of your computer search to your instructor for feedback, circling the references you intend to use and starring the empirical articles.

Be sure to write your research question on the top of your computer search list.

(8)    Select and locate the 10 sources you and your instructor have decided will be most relevant. You should start to track down your literature very soon. Many sources will be available on-line or in your library. Some sources, however, will have to be obtained from another library through Interlibrary Loan, which may require as much as two or three weeks.

(9)    Finally, when you have some literature in hand, among those sources that are most closely related to your research question, choose the most current and examine the authors' references at the end. This will help you identify other relevant sources.

# (B)  Evaluate and Critique the Literature

Your written literature review should summarize and evaluate each author's work as it relates to your study. A literature review is not a series of long, direct quotations, nor is it a list of summaries of each source. Your literature review should integrate and synthesize all of the sources you have selected.

For each source, the following sets of questions will help as you explore the literature. The first set is for use with empirical articles, the second set with nonempirical articles. We have included one blank set of questions for you to use with empirical articles and another for nonempirical articles. We recommend that you photocopy the blank forms for use with additional sources or type the information directly into your computer. We have also included examples for both types of articles.

(1)   For empirical studies:

> Author and Date:
>
> Title:
>
> Citation Information:

> (a)   What is the purpose of this study and how is it related to your study?

> (b)   What theory or theories (if any) does the author use in this study? How might you apply this theory to your topic of study?

(c)   In a brief paragraph describe *how* the sample was
      obtained.

(d)   Include a brief description of the sample (size, gender,
      race, age, socioeconomic class, special characteristics),
      paying close attention to the inclusion and representation
      of people of color, a group frequently underrepresented in
      research. (For example, are people of color included in
      sufficient numbers, or are several groups simply pooled
      together with only white and nonwhite comparisons
      reported? Groups reported as nonwhite do not tell us
      anything about specific minority groups.)

(e)   What are the major concepts in the study and the variables chosen to represent each concept?

(f)   Indicate the specific measures used (operationalization) for each of the major variables in the article that are relevant to your study. Begin with the dependent variables if dependent and independent variables are included. If the article is an evaluation of an intervention, briefly describe the intervention (usually the independent variable).

(g)     Describe the method of data collection.

(h)     Summarize the findings of the study in two or three
        sentences.

(i)    What will you apply from this study to your own? How might you use its strengths or compensate for its limitations?

Sample for Empirical Studies

Author and Date:   Roberts, C.S., Piper, L., Denny, J., & Cuddeback, G. (1997)

Title:   A support group interv. to facilitate young adults' adjust. to cancer

Citation Information:   *Health and Social Work, (22)2*, 133-141.

(a)   What is the purpose of this study and how is it related to your study?

Purpose of the study: to evaluate the effectiveness of an intervention for young cancer patients. The goal of the intervention is to reduce psychological stress and improve coping skills and quality of life.

Relates to my study: I want to evaluate a support group for college students with disabilities. This study (1) evaluates a support group, (2) focuses on young adults (college students are predominantly young adults, so could have similar issues), and (3) uses instruments that may be appropriate for my study.

(b)   What theory or theories (if any) does the author use in this study? How might you apply this theory to your topic of study?

Life-cycle development theory: to understand issues for this population and to develop intervention. Authors point out that younger cancer patients have concerns that are different from older patients.

Group theory: rationale for using standard support group and other group techniques.

Again, both theories are relevant to my study topic and population.

(c)   In a brief paragraph describe *how* the sample was obtained.

Sample was obtained from patients at community hospitals and a cancer center. Social workers explained the group to potential participants and then referred them to the group if they were interested.

NOTE: Actual procedure differed from the initial plan for the study. Authors wanted to find 20 people and conduct a wait-list control group study. They could not find enough people, so they conducted a one-group pretest-posttest design.

Nonprobability sample. All participants received the intervention.

(d)   Include a brief description of the sample (size, gender, race, age, socioeconomic class, special characteristics), paying close attention to the inclusion and representation of people of color, a group frequently underrepresented in research. (For example, are people of color included in sufficient numbers, or are several groups simply pooled together with only white and nonwhite comparisons reported? Groups reported as nonwhite do not tell us anything about specific minority groups.)

Sample size is 14, nine women and five men. Race: 12 were white, one each Native American and African American. Ages ranged from 24 to 34 years old. Nine participants were disabled or unemployed.

Three of 14 people attended three or fewer group sessions and were not included in data analysis.

Small sample, few people of color included.

See article page 134 for more information on demographics.

(e)   What are the major concepts in the study and the variables chosen to represent each concept?

| Major concepts. | Variables. |
|---|---|
| Psychological well-being | tension-anxiety, depression-dejection, anger-hostility, vigor-activity, fatigue-inertia, confusion-bewilderment (subscales on POMS, see below) |
| Coping | coping responses (from WCCL-R, see below) |
| Quality of life | physical, psychosocial, medical interaction, marital, sexual problems (subscales on CARES, see below) |

(f)   Indicate the specific measures used (operationalization) for each of the major variables in the article that are relevant to your study. Begin with the dependent variables if dependent and independent variables are included. If the article is an evaluation of an intervention, briefly describe the intervention (usually the independent variable).

| Dependent Variables: | Measures: |
|---|---|
| tension-anxiety, depression-dejection, anger-hostility, vigor-activity, fatigue-inertia, confusion-bewilderment | Profile of Mood States (POMS) |
| coping responses | Cancer Rehabilitation Evaluation System (CARES) |
| physical, psychosocial, medical interaction, marital, sexual problems | Ways of Coping Checklist (WCCL-R) |
| **Independent Variable:** | Structured, six-week, support group intervention (pp. 135-137) |

(g)     Describe the method of data collection.

Quantitative:
Participants completed scales prior to beginning the group and again one to two weeks after the group ended. Instruments were mailed to participants for them to complete.

Qualitative:
The researcher was a participant-observer at the group meetings and made notes during the groups. Researcher also interviewed group participants to ask them what they found helpful about the group.

(h)     Summarize the findings of the study in two or three sentences.

Quantitative results based on scales: participants indicated an improvement in psychological well-being, but no change in their coping or quality of life.

Qualitative results: participants were asked what was helpful about the group. Areas (themes) related to helpfulness identified: shared experiences, meeting people in same age group, group atmosphere, receiving information.

Authors also combined quantitative and qualitative data to assess the group's goals.

(i)    What will you apply from this study to your own? How might you use its strengths or compensate for its limitations?

Intervention is similar to the intervention I am evaluating, a short-term, structured group.

Intervention uses developmental theory and group theory to explain the rationale for the group and logic for why the group should be effective. Specifically, a younger population of cancer patients faces developmental issues out of "the norm" and may have unique concerns and needs.

My sample size will be small, too, and I may have a similar problem getting enough respondents to have a wait-list control group.

Instruments (POMS and WCCL-R) may be appropriate for my study.

Combines quantitative with qualitative data.

Article does a good job describing the intervention.

Analysis used matched pair t-test. I am not able to asses the appropriateness for my study, will explore further under Data Analysis section.

Authors recommend a longer intervention (8 weeks) so there is time for an introduction and termination session. I think I will have time to do an 8 week group.

Also, authors recommend a closed-session AND time-limited group.

No control group, so authors have to recognize possible threats to internal validity (maturation), which may be true for my study, too.

(2)   For nonempirical articles:

These articles will most likely be expository articles: discussions of theory, summaries of many other studies, or general overviews of the topic you are studying. For each article you plan to use, ask yourself the following questions:

Author and Date:

Title:

Citation Information:

(a)   What is the main topic of this article?

(b)   What information does it provide that is helpful for a better understanding of the topic or helpful in the actual design of your study?

## Sample for Nonempirical Studies

These articles will most likely be expository articles: discussions of theory, summaries of many other studies, or general overviews of the topic you are studying. For each article you plan to use, ask yourself the following questions:

Author and Date:  Fineran, S. & Bennett, L. (1998)

Title: Teenage peer sexual harassment: Implications for social work

practice in education

Citation Information:  *Social Work (43)*1, 55-64.

(a)    What is the main topic of this article?

Sexual harassment. Specifically, peer sexual harassment among youth in school settings. Article discusses history of sexual harassment, reviews empirical literature, and uses theories to assist social workers in school settings.

(b)    What information does it provide that is helpful for a better understanding of the topic or helpful in the actual design of your study?

My study explores reasons why high school students want, or are forced, to attend alternative schools. This article suggests peer sexual harassment as a reason students perform poorly in school or do not want to attend school.

- Defines terms.
- Review of literature on peer sexual harassment.
- Role of social work.
- Theories to help understand sexual harassment.

**Reminder:**

When writing the research proposal, the text is written in future tense, indicating what you will be doing. When writing the final research report, you will have completed the study. The report will describe and explain what you have done, so the report will be written in past tense. If you complete your study, when you write the report, be sure to change the tense to indicate that you have completed the study.

# (C) Write the INTRODUCTION Section

Before you start writing, check with your course instructor for the reference style that she or he expects you to follow. Much social work literature uses the American Psychological Association (APA) reference style. Refer to your APA manual or to the on-line resources available with *Research Navigator Guide*.

You will save much time and energy if you use the expected format and style as you conduct the project and write early drafts. We know from experience that it takes less effort now to put the paper into the correct style than to revise it later. The library, your university's writing center, and on-line resources can provide style manuals to guide you.

Once you have received feedback from your course instructor, you are ready to write the first draft of the introduction and literature review sections of your paper. We say first draft because as you complete the other steps of your study, you may find more information that you want to include.

Both the Introduction section and Literature Review section rely on the sources that you have identified. In the Introduction, you use literature to establish the importance of the topic and the value of your study which will address a gap in the existing literature on the topic. The Introduction also contains a statement clarifying the purpose of the study.

The Introduction section of your paper should be about one page and address the information below. Refer back to Chapter 3: The Research Question for what information to include.

In the space below, outline the scope and significance, relevance, and purpose of your study, identifying the articles that support your points.

✓ Scope and significance of the problem or issue:

✓ Relevance to social work:

✓ Specification of the research question (purpose of the study):

# (D) Write the LITERATURE REVIEW Section

Writing a literature review is difficult for even experienced researchers so don't become discouraged. Most people find synthesizing what they have read to be the most difficult part of the research process. We believe that the best way to learn how to write a good literature review is to read other literature reviews. Reading many literature reviews will help you develop the skills that you need to write a good review. So when you feel stuck, read literature reviews to see how others have organized and presented their literature reviews.

The Literature Review section of your paper provides a context for your study and presents a synthesis and evaluation of prior empirical work on your topic. It justifies the research question you have chosen and the study you will conduct.

Your literature review should use existing literature to:

- Introduce your topic and provide a background for your study
- Describe the context, causes, and responses to the topic you are studying
- Introduce theoretical frameworks
- Define variables and key terms
- Present and critique measures and methods used in prior studies
- Critically review findings of prior empirical work

The final paragraph of your literature review should:

- Summarize and critically evaluate what is currently known about the topic
- Identify contradictory information and gaps in the existing literature
- Restate the purpose of your proposed study

We have provided an example of an annotated literature review on pages 62 through 67 to help you write your literature review.

(1)   Make a plan for how you will present related literature. What are
      the main topics you will cover in your review?

      Organize the topics in a meaningful way so that your discussion
      of the literature has a logical flow. Try beginning with broad,
      general information and move to more specific information. Use
      an expository article to make a particular point and then an
      empirical article to provide evidence for that point.

      Outline the main topics of your literature review on separate
      pages or on your word processor. Once you have the main topic
      areas, you can expand the outline by filling in information from
      your sources. When possible, use multiple sources to support
      your points. Above all, avoid presenting a summary of each
      source one after the other.

(2)   Using your expanded outline as a guide, write your review of the
      literature (minimum of four pages). Use subheadings that match
      your topics to help the reader follow your outline. At the end of
      the literature review state your research question again in its
      final form.

      Keep in mind that as you continue through the workbook and
      the design of your study, you will probably locate other sources
      that you will include in the final draft of your paper.

      Remember that you have an ethical responsibility to cite all your
      sources properly, to indicate when you are using an author's
      exact words, and to make it clear when you are paraphrasing an
      author's ideas. If you are uncertain about proper
      documentation, ask your instructor for assistance or go to your
      university's writing center.

      Submit the drafts of the Introduction and Literature Review
      sections to your course instructor along with your proposed
      study (see Chapter 5: Choosing Your Methodology).

# Annotated Example of a Literature Review

## Introduction

[1] Establishes importance of the issue

[1] Antiretrovirals (ARVs), particularly protease inhibitors, are potent agents in reducing the viral load in HIV-positive individuals. However, these positive effects can be short-lived in many patients if they do not take the antiretroviral medications as prescribed. Poor patient adherence to these drugs can rapidly lead to resistance and negate the benefits of combination therapy. In addition, as a result of poor adherence, public health is threatened as the virus becomes resistant to antiretroviral therapy.

[2] States value of the study

[2] Recent research on adherence to antiretrovirals suggests that adherence rates greater than 90 percent are necessary to maintain suppression of HIV (Patterson et al., 1999). Unfortunately, numerous studies have documented low rates of adherence to antiretroviral medication among HIV-positive individuals (Leslie, 2000). [3] While researchers have sought to determine factors related to adherence among this group, very few efforts have been directed at designing and evaluating approaches to assisting individuals in improving adherence. [2] This area of research is absolutely critical to the development of an effective response to the HIV epidemic (Michael, 2000).

[3] Indicates what is missing from the literature

[4] States purpose of the study

[4] This study seeks to evaluate the effectiveness of a bi-weekly phone counseling approach in increasing adherence to antiretroviral medications among HIV+ persons. [5] The intervention model takes into account individual stages of change readiness and begins the intervention at the patient's level.

[5] Introduces theoretical connection *(additional text removed for the sake of brevity)*

## Background

*HIV in the United States*

[6] Provides context with historical data

[6] Due to improved antiretroviral therapies and treatment, death rates and opportunistic infections associated with AIDS have declined since late 1995, however, the estimated total number of persons living with AIDS has steadily increased. According to the most recent HIV/AIDS Surveillance Report, a total of 665,357 persons with AIDS have been reported to the Centers for Disease Control (CDC) through 30 June 1998. Of these, 401,028 (60%) deaths have been reported. This report indicates that the estimated number of persons living with AIDS is currently greater than 264,000 (Centers for Disease Control and Prevention, 1998).

*Advances in Antiretroviral Therapy*

Several significant advances in the approach to antiretroviral therapy have led to the recently observed changes in the AIDS death rates and incidence of opportunistic infections. Protease inhibitors (PI), a new class of antiretrovirals that attack a different enzyme in the HIV life cycle, are potent agents that can lead to dramatic reductions in the amount of virus in an infected patient's plasma (viral load). Another advance involves the use of combination antiretroviral therapy. As described in the treatment guidelines, it is well established that using a PI in combination with two nucleoside analogs can lead to reduced plasma viral loads, decreased viral resistance, decreased opportunistic infections, increased CD4 or T-cells, and improved survival in many patients. However, these positive effects can be short-lived in many patients if they do not take the antiretroviral medications as prescribed (Vanhove et al., 1996). Poor patient adherence to these drugs can rapidly lead to resistance which negates the clinical benefits of combination therapy. Thus, much attention has been directed to issues of adherence for persons taking antiretrovirals.

*Adherence*

[7] Conceptualization: definition of key terms

[7] *Defining adherence.* Adherence has become a popular term since it may be viewed as less judgmental. However, the terms "compliance" and "adherence" are used interchangeably in the literature (Mehta et al., 1997). As reviewed by Morris and Schulz (1992), patient medication compliance may be defined as a process or an outcome. The outcome-oriented definition is commonly employed by adherence researchers. This approach focuses on a defined outcome as a result of a patient performing a specific action, such as taking medication. It is quantified by the percentage of time that a patient takes her or his medication as prescribed. Currently there is no accepted minimum percentage level or outcome-oriented definition of medication adherence for patients with HIV.

[8] Prior empirical work

[8] *Adherence in chronic illnesses.* Rates of adherence with long term medications for chronic conditions have consistently been found to average around 50%, regardless of illness or setting (Donovan & Blake, 1992). Medication adherence is well studied for chronic disease states such as diabetes, hypertension, tuberculosis, mental illness, and others (Morris & Schulz, 1992).

*Adherence among HIV+ Patients.* Data regarding medication adherence in HIV-infected patients first appeared in the literature in the early 1990s (Samuels et al., 1990). The early studies centered around adherence to single agent antiretroviral regimens involving zidovudine (Samuels et al., 1990; Morse et al., 1991; Samet et al., 1992; Broers et al., 1994; Wall et al., 1995;

Geletko et al., 1996). However, over the past two years there has been renewed interest in evaluating adherence issues in this population due to the increased utilization of combination therapy that requires patients to take complex, multidrug medication regimens with varied dosing schedules. This is a result of, in part, a more complete understanding of viral replication, dynamics, and the development of resistance (Ho, 1996; Mellors et al., 1996). Consideration of practical treatment issue—such as antiretroviral regimens that must be taken indefinitely involving medications that are often times prone to significant adverse effects—has also influenced the renewed interest in evaluating adherence.

*Recent medication adherence studies in HIV patients.* Recent medication studies indicate that 21 to 43% of all patients regularly miss doses of their antiretroviral or opportunistic infection prophylaxis medications. Evidence of nonadherence for a substantial group in this population is currently well documented. More disconcerting are the findings that approximately 40% of treated patients showed detectable viral loads. While the survival benefit provided by these multidrug antiretroviral regimens is impressive, recent findings by Paterson and colleagues (1999) indicate that even >95% adherence resulted in viral suppression for only 81% of patients.

*Measuring Adherence*

[9] **Operationalization: Measures used in prior empirical work**

[9] Adherence typically has been measured both directly and indirectly (Morris & Schulz, 1992). Direct measurements involve detection of certain chemicals in body fluid levels, whereas indirect measures include prescription refills, pill counts, medication self-reports, and even the subjective impressions of health care providers (cf. Morse et al., 1991). Direct measurements, while objective and less biased, may be influenced by individual patient pharmacokinetics and time of medication dosing. Additionally, these methods do not accurately reflect what activity has taken place over time, are generally impractical in many settings, and often lack established reference ranges relative to specific dosing activity.

[10] **Critique of measures**

[10] Indirect measures such as patient interviews and self-reports are among the more common methods; however, they usually overestimate compliance despite the skill of the interviewer or design of the self-report form (Cramer et al., 1989). Prescription refill data and pill counts may be inaccurate since they do not indicate whether medication was taken at prescribed intervals and because patients may discard their medication before a visit to their physician (Scaler et al., 1994). Electronic monitoring is an indirect measure that allows for a more accurate assessment of compliance as compared to pill counts and patient interviews as shown in

numerous studies (Pflomm et al., 1997; Wall et al., 1995; Geletko et al., 1996). However, compliance may still be overestimated since it does not verify the exact dose that was removed from the container or if the medication was actually ingested (Scaler et al., 1994).

*Measuring adherence in HIV+ patients.* A variety of measurement tools have been employed to study medication adherence in HIV-infected patients. Some of these include: questionnaires, diaries, pill count, self report, laboratory/biological markers, antiretroviral plasma assays, physician or study nurse assessments, prescription refill compliance, supervised medication administration, and electronic measuring devices. In a study by Morse et al. (1991), the measure of adherence consisted of nurses' subjective assessments of patient compliance based upon criteria such as appointment-keeping. As shown by concurrent evaluation, and as noted above, most methods greatly overestimate actual medication adherence as compared to electronic monitoring (Pflomm et al., 1997; Wall et al., 1995; Geletko et al., 1996). The majority of studies have utilized a combination of methods to assess medication adherence, a logical approach to measuring adherence since most methods, as discussed above, have inherent limitations.

*Efforts to Improve Adherence*
[11] While it is known that adherence is lower when the regimen is complex and of long duration, requires changes in lifestyle, and is inconvenient and expensive (all factors inherent in antiretroviral medication regimens), there is sparse information regarding the best means of enhancing adherence (Eldred et al., 1997; Urquhart, 1992; Scaler et al., 1994). Most interventions can be categorized as educational, behavioral, or a combination of the two. Educational strategies, involving written and/or verbal communication, are based on an information model of adherence and suggest that patients given sufficient information (regarding the disease, medications, and side effects) will demonstrate increased adherence. Studies of the effectiveness of written information alone have not shown it to be effective in increasing adherence (Mullen et al., 1985). However, a combination of written and verbal information has shown promise, across settings, in increasing adherence and knowledge among adults with hypertension, but with the qualification of specific, focused one-to-one counseling, often provided by a pharmacist (Hussar, 1985; Zismer et al., 1982; Nessman et al., 1980; Cole & Emmanuel, 1971). Noble (1998) notes the importance of physician techniques such as getting the patient involved, widening the discussion, shifting the responsibility

[11] Summarizes what is currently known regarding interventions to improve adherence

back to the patient, educating and empowering the patient, and encouraging full collaboration.

Behavioral interventions, such as medication calendars, refill reminders (by phone or mail), and special medication containers have also increased adherence rates (Morris & Schulz, 1992). Most promising, however, has been the combination of educational and behavioral interventions.

[12] The 1996 review of randomized trials of interventions to improve adherence completed by Haynes, McKibbon, and Kanani stands as the most comprehensive review of that literature to date. Of the 15 RCTs that met their rigorous criteria for inclusion, seven interventions were found to increase adherence levels across clinical problems, including hypertension, asthma, streptococcal throat, epilepsy, and schizophrenia. All but one of those seven involved long-term complex interventions, consisting of various combinations of verbal and written instruction, convenience of care (e.g., simplified dosing), involving patients in their care (e.g., blood pressure monitoring), reminders, and reinforcement. However, the authors concluded that although these complex interventions significantly increased adherence levels, the increases were not significant enough to allow individuals to experience the full benefits of their medications, especially significant in the area of antiretroviral adherence.

Only one study was located that utilized an experimental design to evaluate the effectiveness of an intervention to increase adherence to an antiretroviral, ZDV. Sorenson et al. (1998) evaluated eight weeks of onsite dispensing to 25 patients enrolled in a methadone clinic and compared outcomes to those randomly assigned to a usual care group. The researchers found no statistically significant differences in self-report of adherence during the intervention or at the one month follow-up.

In adherence research it is easy to lose track of the ultimate goal beyond improved adherence, that of clinical benefit. Six of the interventions reviewed by Haynes et al. (1996) resulted in clinical improvement, with only four demonstrating improvement in both adherence and clinical outcome, further emphasizing the researchers' point that the increases in adherence were generally not substantial. Likewise, the Sorenson et al. (1998) study found no significant clinical benefit of onsite dispensing (using mean corpuscular volume as an indicator). Haynes et al. (1996) cited the urgent need for testing of further innovations in treatment methods, innovations that "are more likely to occur if investigators join across clinical disciplines to tackle low adherence" (p. 386).

[12] Critically analyzes findings

## Summary

[13] Reviews key points
of literature review

[13] Near total adherence for individuals taking antiretrovirals is absolutely essential. Unfortunately, only 57-79% of persons taking antiretrovirals achieve adherence levels of 80% or more, a level that most clinicians and researchers realize is unacceptable for this population in its fight against HIV. Equally unfortunate is that, constrained by a relatively short time of investigation, the factors related to adherence have not been well-identified. Neither have the few tests of health behavior models been well supported. Even more unfortunate is that evaluations of efforts to improve adherence among HIV+ individuals have been rare.

[14] Restates purpose of
proposed study

[14] Utilizing a randomized wait-list control group experimental design in two sites, chosen specifically to test the intervention in settings already providing HIV care (a university-based HIV clinic and a community-based pharmacy specializing in HIV care), we intend to:

(1) provide and evaluate services designed to increase levels of adherence among 50 individuals; and

(2) assess risk factors for nonadherence by examining the link between adherence and sociodemographic variables, disease state and perceived risk and threat of illness, intention to adhere, medication regimen, social supports, substance abuse, and emotional health.

Written by Alex Westerfelt, Ph.D. and Melinda Lacy, Pharm.D.

# CHAPTER 5

# CHOOSING YOUR METHODOLOGY & DEVELOPING A TIMELINE

Having examined the literature, you know some of the methods of study others have used to explore your topic. Now you must decide the particular method you will use to conduct your own investigation. This workbook allows for four options: survey research, qualitative research, single-subject design research, and outcomes evaluation.

In most instances, to the extent that you have narrowed and adequately specified your research question, you will have obligated yourself to a particular method of study. If you are uncertain, review your research question. Inherent in most research questions is an indication of the purpose of the research to be undertaken. Remember: Purpose directs method. Ask yourself what the purpose of your study is.

A word about the use of existing data. Many times, agencies have existing data that were previously collected and may be available to you for your study. They might have been collected as part of a survey or program evaluation and not yet analyzed. Using existing data can save time and be less costly than collecting your own. Of course, there are disadvantages to using existing data. Existing data may not have the precise information that you are seeking, may not use the best measure, or may have inaccuracies or missing data that will limit your study.

# (A) Determine the Purpose of Your Study

Check to see which of the following best applies to your question.

❑ If the purpose of your study is to document the magnitude of a problem or the quantity of various characteristics (for example, how satisfied people are with services or how many people need a particular service) or determine individual ratings based on scaled measures (for example, parenting skills), then you will use the survey method. You may also explore existing data that can follow the survey method. In either case, go to Chapter 6.

❑ If the purpose of your study is to gain a deeper understanding of how participants have experienced a particular event or state (for example, homelessness), then qualitative interviewing usually will be your method of choice. This is also true when exploring something about which little is known (for example, how terminally ill cancer patients perceive home visits by social work case managers). Go to Chapter 7.

❑ If the purpose of your study is to evaluate how an intervention affects a single client system (individual, family, program, or community), then single-subject design will most likely be your method of choice. Go to Chapter 8.

❑ If the purpose of your study is to evaluate how an intervention or program affects clients, then an outcomes evaluation is your method of choice. Again, your agency may already have existing data that can be used for an outcomes evaluation. Go to Chapter 9.

This is not to say there is only one right method for each research question. The choice of method depends greatly on the exact specification of what you want to know. Because each research question is unique, we cannot give more specific guidance regarding which method to choose, and we encourage you to talk with your course instructor for further help. Prepare for a discussion with your course instructor by thinking about the purpose of your study and what you have learned from reviewing the literature.

Once you have chosen your method of study, proceed to that chapter of the workbook.

Write a sentence combining the purpose of your study and the method you have chosen below.

| Purpose of Your Study and Method: |
| :-- |
| |

## (B)  Develop Your Proposed Timeline

Now, you should plan for implementing your study. On page 72, we provide a timeline for conducting a research study as part of a one- or two-semester course. You may have more or less time to conduct your study, so plan accordingly.

Enter the dates for completing each stage of your proposed study on the timeline provided on page 72.

## (C)  Submit Proposed Study to Your Course Instructor

Submit drafts of the Introduction and Literature Review sections of your paper along with this chapter (Chapter 5) to your course instructor for his or her feedback.

## Stages of Conducting Your Research Project

**Enter Dates for Completion of Each Stage**

1. **Develop Your Research Question, Plan for Protection of Participants**
   See Workbook Chapters 1, 2, 3, and 11
   _____

2. **Conduct Literature Review, Select Research Design, Determine Sample Design**
   See Workbook Chapters 4, 5, and 10
   _____

3. **Develop Measurement Instruments**
   See Workbook Chapter 6, 7, 8, or 9, depending on your method
   _____

4. **Pilot Measurement Instruments***
   See Workbook Chapter 6, 7, 8, or 9, depending on your method
   _____

5. **Collect Your Data**
   See Workbook Chapter 6, 7, 8, or 9, depending on your method
   _____

6. **Analyze Your Data**
   See Workbook Chapters 12, 13, or 14, depending on your method
   _____

7. **Prepare Final Research Report**
   See Workbook Chapter 15
   _____

**Submit Final Research Report**    _____

_* Remember, you must have IRB approval even before piloting your instrument_

# CHAPTER 6

# SURVEY RESEARCH

**Recommended Article:**
Marino, R., Green, R., & Young, E. (1998). Beyond the scientist-practitioner model's failure to thrive: Social workers' participation in agency-based research activities. *Social Work Research*, 22(3), 188-192.

Researchers rely more on survey methods than any other method. With appropriate sampling procedures, researchers utilize survey methods to gather a wealth of information about individuals, families, groups, and communities. Options for the design of survey studies are addressed below. This chapter of the workbook is intended to guide you through each of the steps necessary to design a survey study.

Now that you have completed a review of the literature, you are ready to develop a research instrument and plan its method of administration.

## (A) Translate Concepts and Variables into Measures

**Reminder:**
Review your methods text regarding operationalization and measurement.

In your literature review you identified major concepts and variables from other studies and indicated the measures (indicators) chosen for each of them. Now you will develop the indicators for each variable you intend to measure.

In the case of scales that are used in studies and cited in articles, you may have to locate another article that contains the actual items of the scale and includes information about the development and testing of that scale. The other article will be listed in the references of the study article you have read. Sometimes you may need to call or write the author to see the actual scale. Some scales are copyrighted and can be used only if a fee is paid for its use. If you plan to use an existing scale, allow time to find these things out and obtain a copy of the scale.

In addition to what you find in your literature review, there are other resources available to you. Your agency may have instruments that are available for your use. There are also texts which include many scales such as Fischer and Corcoran's (1994) *Measures for Clinical Practice* and Jordan and Franklin's (2004) *Clinical Assessment for Social Workers*. These usually can be found in your library's reference section. For additional suggestions for texts with existing scales, see Rubin and Babbie's (2005) *Research Methods for Social Work*.

If, on the other hand, you develop your own instrumentation, allow time to share it with others and receive feedback.

(1)   What are the key variables of interest in your study?

Drawing from your literature review, how have others measured each of these?

On the following page, specify each variable, then complete the information in the table.

If the agency has measured these variables before, include those measures or questions here.

| Variable Author & Date | Measure | Brief Description | Scale Reliability & Validity | How Collected & Time Involved |
|---|---|---|---|---|
| (1) | | | | |
| (2) | | | | |
| (3) | | | | |

(2)    Your intended measures:

    (a)    On the preceding page, circle the measures that you plan to use. You may choose more than one. If you do not plan to use any of these measures, go to Part (b). If you plan to use one or more scales, check the original source on each scale, and indicate how much time it will take to complete the measure, either by interview or self-administered.

    (b)    If none of the above measures seems appropriate, or if you want to develop measures of your own in addition to conventional measures you have selected, indicate why.

    (c)    What measure(s) do you propose?

(d)     Evaluate whether the above measures have a cultural bias in terms of age; race; gender; social class; physical, mental or emotional ability; or sexual orientation. In the case of validated scales, with whom and with what age group have the scales been tested for validity and reliability?

(e)     Discuss potential limitations of your measures relative to reliability and validity.

# (B) Construct Your Research Questionnaire

## Reminder:

Review your text regarding construction of questionnaires.

You are now ready to construct the questionnaire for your study. The measures you have detailed above will make up part of the questionnaire, but you will probably want to include other items as well. The following questions are intended to help you further develop the questionnaire.

(1)   Check with agency staff and see what other questions they would like to include. Indicate to whom you talked and their ideas.

(2)     What other questions would clients like to include? Indicate to whom you talked and their ideas.

(3)     Indicate basic, relevant information you wish to collect, such as age, race, gender, or social class.

(4)     On separate pages, draft a copy of your questionnaire, including each question word-for-word, in the order you intend to present the items.

(5)    Refine each item on the questionnaire to accomplish the following:

❑ For close-ended questions, exhaustive and mutually exclusive responses.
❑ No double-barreled questions.
❑ No biased items or terms.
❑ No leading questions.
❑ Clear instructions if questionnaire is to be self-administered.

(6)    Revise your draft so that you can answer "yes" to the following questions, placing a check in the space when you meet the criterion.

❑ Is the questionnaire uncluttered?
❑ Is it as brief as possible?
❑ Is the order of questions appropriate (first questions capture the participant's interest; sensitive questions come later)?
❑ Are appropriate "skip" questions used so that people are not asked irrelevant questions?
❑ Have you formatted the questionnaire in a way that will be easy for you to analyze and tabulate?
❑ Is the language appropriate for the participants?
❑ At what reading level is your questionnaire written? (Use your word processor for an analysis of reading level.)

(7)    Give the questionnaire to two others to critique (your field instructor, other agency staff, peers).

(8)    On a separate page, produce a "clean" version of your questionnaire, incorporating the feedback you received from others.

(9)    Submit your draft questionnaire to your course instructor to approve before you pilot it. Include a synopsis of your research instrument, including the topics it covers.

# (C) Plan How to Administer Your Questionnaire

## Reminder:
Review your text regarding options for
administering questionnaires.

Survey research can be conducted in several ways. You must decide if the questionnaire will be self-administered by the participant or administered by an interviewer who will record the participant's responses. Also, you must decide whether you will distribute the questionnaire in person to the participants or mail it to them.

Complete the following questions. Some may not apply to you depending on the method of administration you choose. Simply skip those questions and go to the next set.

*If the questionnaire is to be self-administered (as opposed to completed by an interviewer) and distributed by the researcher or an assistant (as opposed to distributed by mail):*

(1)   When, where, and how will the questionnaire be distributed? By whom? Will it be distributed to individuals or groups? Justify your choices.

(2)   List the information that the person who distributes the questionnaire will give to the participant.

(3)   Will the questionnaire be anonymous or confidential? Include your rationale for the option you have chosen.

(4)     What are the conditions for questionnaire completion and
        return? Completed on the spot or returned later? If later, how
        will participants be instructed to return the questionnaires?
        What is the final date for returning the questionnaires? What is
        your plan for follow-up of unreturned questionnaires? Justify
        your choices.

(5)     What are your plans to enhance your response rate? Anticipate
        and list here some reasons people might give for not completing
        the questionnaire and how you plan to respond to those.

(6)     Describe any compensation to the participants for their time and expenses and the procedure for compensation. (Federal rules on research stipulate that you cannot offer incentives to participants, but you can compensate them for their time.)

(7)     What are your procedures for handling a situation where an individual starts but does not complete the questionnaire?

(8)     What will be your process for reviewing a questionnaire for missed responses by the participant?

*If the questionnaire is to be self-administered*
*and distributed by mail:*

(1)   Will the questionnaire be anonymous or confidential? Include
      your rationale for the option you have chosen.

(2)   On separate pages, outline a cover letter including the following:
      a persuasive introduction regarding importance and purpose of
      the study; who is sponsoring the research; how the sample was
      selected; a statement that participation is voluntary and will not
      affect services for which the participant is eligible; assurance of
      anonymity or confidentiality; the estimated time for completion
      of the questionnaire; directions for return of the questionnaire
      and the cutoff date for return of the questionnaire.

      Remember to keep your letter short and clear. Consider using
      bullet points. Sentences should be free of jargon and short in
      length. Aim for a 7th grade reading level for your consent form.

(3)     Indicate whether you plan to use stamped return envelopes or business reply envelopes and why.

(4)     Indicate your plans and dates regarding follow-up mailings, if any. What is the estimated total cost for your mailing?

(5)  Describe any compensation to the participants for their time and expenses and the procedure for compensation. (Federal rules on research stipulate that you cannot offer incentives to participants, but you can compensate them for their time.)

*If the questionnaire will be completed by an interviewer:*

(1)   When and where will the interviews be conducted? By whom?

(2)   List the information that the interviewer will give to the participant prior to starting the interview.

(3)   What are your plans to enhance your response rate; i.e., to persuade people to agree to be interviewed? Anticipate and list some reasons people might give for not completing the questionnaire and how you plan to respond to those.

(4)     Describe any compensation to the participants for their time and expenses and the procedure for compensation. (Federal rules on research stipulate that you cannot offer incentives to participants, but you can compensate them for their time and other expenses they incur, such as travel and child care.)

(5)     What are your procedures for handling a situation where an individual starts but does not complete the interview?

# (D) Pilot Your Research Instrument and Plan for Data Collection

The validity and reliability of your questionnaire can be greatly enhanced by piloting it prior to your actual data collection. This also helps you anticipate any problems related to administration. *You must obtain approval from the IRB and agency personnel before piloting your interview with clients.*

(1)    Pilot your instrument, making conditions as similar as possible to those you expect during data collection. Use agency staff, classmates, and clients of the agency who would not eventually receive the questionnaire.

(2)    Indicate with whom you piloted your instrument and the results of the pilots. Discuss questions that were problematic for people, variations in length of time to administer, logistical problems regarding where and how the interviews were conducted, and any problems with administering the consent form.

(3)     Indicate below the changes you will make in the administration of your study, based on the results of your pilot.

(4)     Now revise your questionnaire and have your course instructor approve the final version.

## (E)  Write the METHODS Section

Again, this will be a first draft of this section of your paper. As you proceed through the following steps, you may return to this section and make revisions. This section will vary in length according to how many measures you have chosen. You can expect this section of the paper to be roughly two to three pages. It should include the following information:

- Each major variable, starting with the dependent variable, if applicable
- The chosen measure(s) for each variable and use in prior studies
- Validity and reliability of each measure
- A brief overview of pilot efforts
- Details of plans for administration of the questionnaire
- Consent procedures and protection of data

## (F)  Data Collection

Data collection should follow the plan you set out in this section. Once you have completed data collection, you will revise the methods section to report how you actually collected the data.

# CHAPTER 7

# QUALITATIVE RESEARCH

**Recommended Article:**
Siegel, D. H. (2003). Open adoption of infants: Adoptive parents' feelings seven years later. *Social Work, 48*(3), 409-419.

The goal of qualitative research is to study a problem in-depth and in detail from the perspective of the research participants in order to understand the meanings people give to situations and experiences. In qualitative research the data are textual rather than numerical.

Qualitative studies are similar to social work case studies and seek to understand what people believe and feel about a particular problem, situation, or program. Social workers often find qualitative research interviewing to be similar to interviewing clients in practice. The goals, however, are different. In practice, our goal is to help clients with their problems and concerns. In qualitative research, our goal is to obtain information that can help us answer our research question.

Qualitative studies help us understand a problem or situation by focusing on a small number of people's experiences. Program evaluations, needs assessments, and client satisfaction studies can be conducted using qualitative methods as well. Data for qualitative studies are most often collected through interviewing, by observation, and from existing documents such as agency documents and newspaper articles. Although there are several methods for collecting qualitative data, we focus solely on structured or semi-structured interviewing with individuals or groups. Structured and semi-structured interviews both have specific open-ended questions that are asked of each participant. This format permits comparisons among the participants and data that are easier to analyze than data from unstructured interviews. Unstructured qualitative interviews should be left to experienced researchers.

Qualitative methods are not easier than quantitative methods just because you don't have to "do" statistics. After completing the interviews, the researcher must analyze and synthesize textual rather than numerical data. Qualitative analysis requires rigorous analytical thinking and the ability to convey that in written form.

Keep in mind: The perspectives of the research participants are of utmost importance and relevance to a qualitative study.

## Reminder:

Review a text devoted to qualitative methods. A general research text may not provide enough information to help you conduct a good qualitative study.

# (A) Develop the Interview Agenda: Your Research Instrument

Begin by reviewing your research question and your rationale for deciding to conduct a qualitative study. Qualitative research questions are generally not as precise as quantitative questions. However, you must have a good understanding of your topic, the focus of your study, and who your research participants will be. The section on *nonprobability samples* in Chapter 10, Sample Design, will help you plan how you will select your sample. Qualitative methods texts present more detailed information that will help you select a sample and develop your interview agenda.

(1)   Develop a list of demographic and other general information you want to collect for each participant (e.g., age, race, gender, or social class). List these below.

(2)  Refer to your literature review to remind yourself what others studying your topic found. Write here the specific topics they included in their studies.

(3)  Now, generate a list of the topics that relate directly to your research question. Use what you learned from the literature review and your own personal experiences with the population and area you are studying. Stay focused on your research question. There will by many areas related to your topic, but you will not have time to explore them all.  List the general topics you want to cover below.

(4)   Ask your field instructor, other agency staff, clients, and your peers for their suggestions regarding topics to include in the interviews. List to whom you talked and their suggestions.

(5)   From your research topics, develop eight to ten open-ended questions on a separate page. These questions should solicit information to answer your research question. Don't worry about the order of the questions at this point, but you should pay special attention to the wording. Questions should be focused, yet broad enough to allow the participants to share their perspectives. Avoid biases of age; race; gender; social class; physical, mental, or emotional ability; or sexual orientation. Use a separate page to write your questions.

(6)     Now, add key points that you want to cover under each of the main questions that you have developed. These points will provide guidance for the interviewer (even if you are the only interviewer) and ensure that you ask the same questions of all participants.

(7)     Draft your interview agenda on separate pages, putting your questions and key points under each one, into a format that follows a logical order. Questions should move from general to specific and from less sensitive to more sensitive topics. The interview format should make sense to your participants *and* allow you to stay focused while collecting data.

Circulate the draft of your interview agenda to the people who helped you generate questions and to other individuals as well. Obtain their feedback and revise your interview agenda. List here with whom you talked, their titles or roles, and the feedback they gave.

| Name: | Feedback: |
| --- | --- |
|  |  |

# (B)  Plan How to Conduct Interviews

**Reminder:**
Refer to a qualitative methods text for information about conducting in-depth interviews with individuals or in a group setting (focus groups).

(1)    Indicate whether you will conduct individual or group interviews. Give the rationale for your choice. When conducting group interviews, remind yourself to hear from each participant and don't expect agreement among participants.

(2)    How and where will the interviews be scheduled? Locate a quiet, comfortable place in which you can avoid interruptions and that allows for confidentiality.

(3)   What will you need to conduct the interview? How will you record the data? Tape recording with an audio cassette recorder and having your tapes transcribed verbatim is one method. However, you may not have the resources for this. (One hour of interview time takes at least three to four hours to transcribe and can result in 30 pages or more of typed data.) Other means of recording qualitative interview data include: 1) taping with partial transcribing, 2) taping and later taking notes while listening to the tapes, and 3) taking extensive notes during and after the interviews when recording is not possible. It is helpful to include another person as notetaker so you can focus on the interview.  Notes taken before, during, and after the interviews are commonly referred to as field notes.

(4)   Indicate who will conduct the interviews. If there is more than one interviewer, how will you prepare the interviewers so that the interviews are conducted consistently? Specify the training and supervision interviewers will receive.

(5)   Describe any compensation to the participants for their time and expenses and the procedure for compensation. (Federal rules on research stipulate that you cannot offer incentives to participants, but you can compensate them for their time and other expenses they incur, such as travel and child care.)

(6)   List the information you will give to the participant just prior to the start of the interview. Include the purpose of the interview, how long it will take, and explain how you will record the data. Remember to also have the participant read and sign the consent form prior to the interview.

(7)   On a separate page, write the information into a script that the interviewer can read to participants before beginning the interviews.

(8)     What are your procedures for handling a situation where an
        individual starts but does not complete the interview?

(9)     Indicate your plan for handling a situation in which an
        individual becomes upset during the interview.

## (C) Pilot Your Interview Agenda and Plan for Data Collection

Piloting your interview can help you identify and remedy potential problems in data collection. *You must obtain approval from IRB and agency personnel before piloting your interview with clients.* Coordinate this through your course instructor and field instructor.

(1) Pilot your interview agenda making conditions as similar as possible to those you expect during data collection. You may interview agency staff, classmates, or clients who would not eventually be interviewed for your study.

(2) Indicate with whom you piloted the interview and how long the interview took; include their feedback. Add your own ideas regarding what you think worked well and what you would like to change.

(3) Revise your interview agenda using your experience and the feedback from the participants with whom you piloted the instrument. Obtain final approval of the interview agenda from your field instructor and course instructor.

## (D)  Write the METHODS Section

In the first draft of this section (roughly two to three pages), you should include the following:

- How you developed the interview agenda
- Whether you will conduct individual or group interviews
- How you plan to record the data
- Who will conduct the interviews and how they will be trained
- Results of your pilot efforts
- Consent procedures and protection of data

## (E)  Data Collection

Data collection should follow the plan you set out in this section. Once you have completed data collection, you will revise the methods section to report how you actually collected the data.

# CHAPTER 8

# SINGLE-SUBJECT DESIGN RESEARCH

---

**Recommended Article:**

Brophy, G. (2000). Social work treatment of sleep disturbance in a 5-year-old boy: A single-case evaluation. *Research on Social Work Practice, (10)*6, 749-760.

---

Single-*subject* design is also referred to as single-*system* design, reflecting its applicability to any client system—a single individual, a single family, a single program, a single community. We assume that most students using this design will choose a single individual as the client system. We have developed the material with that in mind. It is not difficult, however, to adapt and complete this chapter with a different client system in mind, and we encourage you not to overlook other client systems when considering your options.

Single-subject research is a frequently utilized method of evaluating one's practice. Its implementation parallels many of the activities of good practice. It allows you to evaluate your practice while at the same time it provides a system for ongoing feedback to both you and your client on how well your work is progressing. Single-subject design requires the selection of measures that can be collected frequently (daily or weekly at least) so that you can record and visually examine progress on a graph.

Single-subject design is inherently a causal study asking whether an intervention is effective. In other words, to what extent does the intervention cause a change in the client. As such, it requires the researcher to be aware of the internal and external validity limitations of the design. We encourage you to review this aspect of single-subject design as you plan your study.

This chapter of the workbook is intended to guide you through the steps of designing a single-subject study. First you must determine whether your client is willing to participate in your research study. Review a copy of the consent form with the client. (The consent form is developed in Chapter 11.) Be sure that your client does not feel pressured to participate and understands that refusal to participate will not affect receipt of or eligibility for agency services.

# (A) Translate Concepts into Variables

## Reminder:

Review single-subject design in a methods text and review your methods text regarding operationalization and measurement.

In your literature review you identified major concepts and variables from other studies and indicated the measures (indicators) chosen for each of them. Now you will specify the indicators for each variable you intend to measure.

In single-subject design studies, the dependent variable is the target goal chosen by the client and worker. These target goals should be reflected in the case plan that you have developed with the client.  One of the advantages of a single subject design is that it can be tied directly to and strengthen the case plan. As you complete these steps, you may find yourself returning to the case plan and making changes that will clarify what you and your client are working on. What are the goals that your client is interested in pursing? Your literature review should reflect material on your goals. Keep in mind that more than one target goal may be chosen.

List here two or three goals (variables or outcome measures) that you and your client have chosen.

# (B) Translate Variables into Measures (Operationalization)

There are three broad categories of sources for finding measures: questions or scales currently used by the agency, questions or scales you find in the literature, and your own creations. One advantage of the literature review you did earlier is that it will give you a sense of how others have defined and measured outcomes relative to the issues your intervention addresses.

The important issue in single subject design is that you select measures that will reveal changes over short periods of time. There are some obvious measures that easily meet these criteria such as number of classes missed each day, number of tantrums per day, number of days attending school per week. If these measures fit for your chosen goals, they will work well for a single subject design. However, sometimes you will need to use less obvious measures. For example, perhaps you want to evaluate your work with a child on reducing his overall level of aggression in his interactions with peers, and it is not feasible for school personnel to keep track of his interactions on a daily basis.

In the literature you might find an evaluation of an intervention designed to reduce aggressive behavior in elementary school youth. Perhaps the school social worker conducted a nine-week group for targeted youth, and the researchers found that at posttest the youth scored better on an aggression scale as compared to their baseline scores. You might decide that the aggression scale is perfect of your purposes. However, if your study is a single subject design, what you must first determine is whether the scale is sensitive enough to show change over a short period of time. You would want to be able to administer the scale weekly to your client and put the scale score on a graph showing progress from week to week. You will have to do some further research on the scale to determine if it will fit those purposes.

In the case of scales that are used in studies and cited in articles, you may have to locate another article that contains the actual items of the scale and includes information about the development and testing of that scale. The other article will be listed in the references of the study article you read.

Sometimes you may need to call or write the author to see the actual scale. Some scales are copyrighted and can be used only if a fee is paid for each one used. If you plan to use an existing scale, allow time to research these things and obtain a copy of the scale.

In addition to what you have found in your literature review, there are other resources available to you. Your agency may have instruments that are available for your use. There are also texts that include multiple scales such as Fischer and Corcoran's (1994) *Measures for Clinical Practice* and Jordan and Franklin's (2004) *Clinical Assessment for Social Workers*. These usually can be found in your library's reference section. For more suggestions for texts on existing scales, see Rubin and Babbie's (2005) *Research Methods for Social Work*.

If, on the other hand, you develop your own instrumentation, allow time to share it with others and receive feedback.

(1)   What are the dependent variables (outcomes) you are considering?

(2)   Drawing from your literature review, how have others measured each of these?

Specify each outcome variable you are considering in the table on the following page. If the agency has measured these variables before, also include their measures or questions in the table.

(3)   Your intended measures:

    (a)   Star each of the measures you plan to use and indicate why. You may choose more than one. (If you do not plan to use any of the measures, go to Part (b.) Now, go to (e).

    (b)   If none of the measures you have identified seems appropriate, or if you want to develop measures of your own in addition to conventional measures you have selected, indicate why.

    (c)   What measure(s) do you propose?

## Outcome Measures (Dependent Variables)

| | Article 1 | Article 2 |
|---|---|---|
| Author/Date | | |
| Measure | | |
| Description | | |
| Reliability/Validity | | |
| Who Collected, How Often, Time Involved | | |
| Sensitive to Change Over Short Period of Time? (Yes/No) | | |

(d)    Evaluate whether these measures have a cultural bias in terms of age; race; gender; social class; physical, mental or emotional ability; or sexual orientation. In the case of validated scales, with whom and with what age group have the scales been tested for validity and reliability?

(e)    Discuss potential limitations of your measures relative to reliability and validity.

(4)   Other considerations for your measures:

    (a)   Regardless of the measure(s) you have chosen, what will be your data source? Some of your options include using available records, doing interviews, direct observation, and self-reporting (including the use of logs and journals).

    (b)   Who will be responsible for collecting the data? What is the potential for reactivity, obtrusiveness, and social desirability biases?

(c)     Consider each of the following questions to finalize your choice of measures:

     ✓ To what extent are the measures sensitive to small, short-term changes?

     ✓ Are or can the indicators be phrased positively?

     ✓ For the target goals, will you measure frequency, duration, magnitude, or a combination?

(5)    Indicate how you will triangulate the target goal measures.

(6)    Specify what your intervention will be (location, specific activities, duration, frequency).

# (C) Identify the Specific Single-Subject Design

Your choice of design will depend on what is practical in your agency and with your client, the nature of the intervention (varying intensity, multiple components, irreversible effects) and the chosen target goals. At a minimum, you should use an AB design, expanding on it as possible.

(1)     Graph:

Sketch out a simple graph of an AB design. Mark the X-axis with the range of scores for the selected target goal and the Y-axis with the intended observation points. Draw a vertical line across the Y-axis at the point where you intend to begin the intervention, demarcating the baseline and intervention phases.

Evaluate your design with attention to these questions.

 (2)    Baseline phase:

  ✓ Do you have enough measurement points that a stable
    baseline can be established (five to ten points)?

  ✓ If it is not feasible to collect baseline date, how can you use
    retrospective data for construction of the baseline?

  ✓ Can you use multiple baselines, either for different target
    goals or with different clients?

 (3)    Intervention phase:

  ✓ Do you intend to withdraw the intervention for some period of
    time and then provide it again (an ABAB design)? Indicate
    when and how on the graph.

  ✓ Do you have an intervention that will be offered in changing
    intensity (an $AB^1B^2B^3$ design)? Explain and add to the graph.

  ✓ Do you have an intervention with several components (an
    ABCD design)? Specify on your graph.

(4)    Would it be possible to do more than one single-subject study; i.e., use the same design with more than one client? Explain.

(5)    Indicate the limitations relative to internal validity. (See pages 136-137 for a review of threats to internal validity.)

(6)    Indicate the limitations relative to external validity.

## (D)  Write the METHODS Section

Again, this will be a first draft of this section because, as you proceed through the other steps, you may return and make revisions. This section will vary in length according to how many measures you have chosen. It should include (roughly one to two pages) the following information:

- Dependent variables (the target goals) and the client's input
- The chosen measure(s) for each variable and use in prior studies
- The validity and reliability of each measure
- The independent variable (the intervention)
- Details on the chosen design, rationale, and limitations
- Consent form and protection of data

## (E)  Data Collection

Data collection should follow the plan you set out in this section. Once you have completed data collection, you will revise the methods section to report how you actually collected the data.

### Note:

Because single-subject designs use an "N of 1," you do not need to complete Chapter 10 of the workbook (Sample Design), and you should disregard references to the sample when writing the final report in Chapter 15. You should, however, give a brief synopsis of the client situation and the circumstances that led to that person's choice of goals. Proceed to Chapter 14.

# CHAPTER 9

# OUTCOMES EVALUATION

---

**Recommended Article:**
Roberts, C., Piper, L., Denny, J., & Cuddeback, G. (1997). A support group intervention to facilitate young adults' adjustment to cancer. *Health and Social Work, 22,* 133-141.

---

Another field of research is called program evaluation, of which there are several types. Process evaluation and outcomes evaluation are the two most common types of program evaluation.

Funders will often require a *process* evaluation as part of a funding agreement. While we do not provide a chapter on process evaluation in this workbook, we mention it here to clarify how it fits with program evaluation and because we want to point out its usefulness as a research product.

A process evaluation may precede or occur simultaneously with an outcomes evaluation. The focus of a process evaluation is in essence the telling of the story of how an agency implements a program and/or evaluation. Imagine you read great things about a program that is meeting the needs of the same population that your agency serves and you want to start a similar program. What is the most useful information you could obtain? Probably answers to questions such as: What exactly did they do? What staffing and training did they have? What problems did they encounter? What did they fail to anticipate when they started? How did they handle the challenges of getting the program up and running? What would they recommend to others? *That* is a process evaluation. Another way to conceive of a process evaluation is to imagine a reporter chronicling the development and implementation of a program from day one until the day that it has been fully implemented.

Outcomes evaluation is another type of program evaluation. Some researchers make a distinction between outcomes *evaluation* and outcomes *monitoring.* In both types, we are interested in specifying the intended outcomes of a program. In outcomes monitoring, the focus is on tracking the outcome results over time. In outcomes evaluation, the focus is on demonstrating that the intervention is responsible for achieving the intended outcomes.

An outcomes monitoring project is often chosen rather than an outcomes evaluation because an agency or program is just beginning to do research. The staff want to begin with something smaller and more manageable. In other instances, it may be impractical or too difficult to develop the control or comparison group that is required for comparing people receiving the intervention to those not receiving it (outcomes evaluation). Only with a control or comparison group can you determine if the changes found are the result of your program. You will be able to use this chapter of the workbook for either an outcomes monitoring study or an outcomes evaluation study.

You may remember from your research methods class a research design called the *one group pretest-posttest design.* We will discuss design issues in more detail in section C, but for now we want to note that the *one group pretest-posttest design* is the type of design used in an outcomes monitoring study. Outcomes are measured at baseline and follow-up for one group of clients. This allows you to determine if changes in the outcomes measures have occurred. You will not be able to claim, however, that the program was responsible for the change.

The United Way has developed an excellent resource for agencies to use when engaging in outcomes measurement. The manual is simple, basic, and geared to beginners. It contains many examples of outcome statements and outcome measures applied to several different types of programs. We encourage you to examine *Measuring Program Outcomes: A Practical Approach* (1996), often available through your local United Way or by calling Sales Service/America at 800-772-0008 and asking for item number 0989.

Evaluating the extent to which a program or intervention causes the intended outcomes has become increasingly important as more funding sources require outcomes evaluations. However, outcomes evaluation has its own intrinsic rewards. Programs can benefit simply from the process of designing an evaluation when providers take the time to consider the "match" between their services and the intended outcomes. What can we realistically expect to happen as a result of this program? This is often referred to as the logic or rationale behind a program, and evaluators will sometimes speak in terms of a "logic model."

For example, objectives for a therapeutic arts program in a juvenile detention facility include the reduction of aggressive behaviors, and in the long run, a lower rate of recidivism. But should an arts program meeting two hours a week for ten weeks be expected to have these results? The program directors realized that such a limited experience in the context of so many influences in a teen's life was unlikely to have a major impact on whether or not the teen committed future delinquent offenses. Further, as the program directors explained the rationale behind their program, they fully expected that the program, if successful, might initially *increase* acting out behaviors of youth as they began to confront issues in their lives. Simply the *process* of designing an evaluation of their program was helpful to them as they thought through the rationale behind their intervention (the logic) and what they sought to accomplish (the outcomes) with it.

- In section A we will guide you through the process of specifying the *logic model* behind your intervention. Laying out the rationale or logic for an intervention and clarifying the link between the intervention and the program's objectives or goals will answer the question of *why* we can expect clients to change as a result of receiving the intervention.

- The next task in an outcomes evaluation is to specify the *program outcomes and their measures* (section B). Sometimes programs have stated objectives that lend themselves more easily to the development of outcome measures. Other times, when the objectives are more general or unwritten, the development of outcome measures takes more thought. We guide you through the various steps for constructing solid outcome measures.

- The third task in designing your study is development of a plan for when and how the data will be collected. We refer you back to Chapter 6, Survey Research, where we provide a series of questions to help you incorporate the necessary considerations for specifying your *data collection procedures.*

- The fourth task involves developing how you can demonstrate that the observed change is a result of the intervention and not other factors in the clients' lives—internal validity (section C). This is the task of *research design,* and we provide three different designs commonly used to evaluate programs (one group pretest-posttest, comparison group, and control group design) and guide you through the process of choosing one.

- The final task is to specify your sample design (section D).

At the end of this chapter on pages 143-144, we provide an example of an outcomes evaluation—Logic Model—of the Quest Program, a program designed to improve adherence to a medication regimen. You may find it helpful to review the example before continuing on in this chapter, and then once again after reviewing the material in this chapter.

## (A) Developing the Rationale for the Intervention: A Logic Model

(1)     Specify what your program is supposed to do. Describe the program in terms of targeted problems, services delivered (type, frequency, and duration), who provides the services, and where the services are provided. Provide a thorough but succinct description. This will clarify the specific components of your program that you expect to facilitate change for your clients.

(2)    What are the stated goals or outcomes of the program? (Goals and outcomes are not necessarily the same thing. We will clarify the distinction in a later step. For now, state in general terms what the program is trying to accomplish.) The goals may be written in program literature (brochures, reports for funding sources, grants) or they may not be written, in which case you will need to seek clarification from agency staff.

(3)    Explain the rationale linking the intervention with the goals you have identified. Another way to think of this is to imagine you are explaining to a friend why your intervention or program *should* accomplish the goals of the program.

# (B) Developing Program Outcomes and their Measures

## Reminder:
Review your methods text regarding operationalization and measurement.

If you have ever been confused about the distinction between goals, objectives, targets, benchmarks, outcomes, measures, and indicators, rest assured you are not alone. Because there is no commonly accepted set of definitions for these terms, it is one of the most confusing areas in evaluation research. If one of the tasks in learning to do research can be likened to learning a foreign language, evaluation research is even more difficult because everyone is not speaking the same language. How the terms are defined and used varies from author to author.

Our advice is this: If you are writing a grant proposal or providing a project report to a funding source, use their definitions. If they do not provide any, determine if they have specific definitions in mind. If not, either use the terms you already know or use ours. We provide some easy definitions and examples below.

*Goals* are broad general statements about the desired results of a program.
- Program Goal: To improve social skills

*Outcomes* are more specific statements about what the program intends to accomplish, what *change* it hopes to achieve. (Objectives can often serve as outcome statements as well. Sometimes people will use "Impact Statement" to refer to an outcome.)
- Program Outcome (Objective): To reduce the number of aggressive incidents in the group home and at school

When developing outcomes, keep in mind that the outcome must indicate change—in knowledge, attitudes, behavior, condition, or status (e.g., from danger to safety in housing condition). If the outcome does not indicate change, it is probably what others refer to as an *output* or a *product* of the program. Agencies generally measure outputs such as number of clients served, hours of service provided, and/or client satisfaction. These are *not* outcomes. (An exception to this would be programs that provide emergency services only, such as shelters, food pantries, and meal programs. The intended outcome in this instance is the commodity provided; the program does not seek to facilitate change in the client.)

*Indicators or measures* are the specific data items that are used to determine if the outcomes (or objectives) have been accomplished.
- Program Measure: Number of incident reports

*Targets* are simply that, targets for the outcome to achieve.
- Program Target: To have 20 or fewer incident reports in the next quarter

*Benchmarks* are simply another type of target, one to beat. People may use last year's final measure (e.g. In the prior calendar year we averaged 20 incident reports a quarter) or a measure from a similar program (e.g. Group homes in the region reported an average of 20 incident reports per quarter).

The following steps will guide you through the process of specifying your outcomes.

(1)   Identify the outcomes of your program. There may be more than one and outcomes may be linked to each other. For example, increases in *knowledge* about HIV/AIDS promotes safer sex *behavior* (further defined as condom use) which in term leads to a reduction in the rate of infection in a community (*condition*). A program may seek to accomplish all of those outcomes; however, for the purposes of your study, you might select only two of them for evaluation, depending upon your purpose, time, and money available for the study.

If this is your first study, keep it simple: choose two or three outcomes to measure. The outcomes may be identified for you already in the program literature. If not, you will need to develop the specific outcome statements for your program. Use this checklist to evaluate and strengthen your outcome statements.

Outcome statements:

✓ Reflect change in client behavior, skills, attitudes, knowledge, or condition.

✓ Follow logically from what the program is trying to accomplish and all stakeholders would agree (clients, staff, funders).

✓ Are reasonable expectations for measurable change within the timeframe of the study?

Once you have identified the intended program outcomes, the next step is to specify how to measure your outcomes. How will you know if the intended changes occurred? What evidence will you have that indicates change?

There are three broad categories of sources for finding measures: 1) questions or scales currently used by the agency, 2) questions or scales you find in the literature, and 3) your own creations. One advantage of the literature review you conducted earlier is that you have a sense of how others have defined and measured outcomes relative to the issues your intervention addresses.

In the case of scales used in studies and cited in articles, you may have to locate another article that contains the actual items of the scale and includes information about the development and testing of that scale. Check the references for the original article. You may call or write the author to see the actual scale and gain permission to use it. Some scales are copyrighted and a fee is charged for their use. If you plan to use an existing scale, allow time to obtain permission to use the scale.

In addition scales and measures found in your literature review, your agency may also have instruments that are available for your use. In addition, check for texts that include multiple scales such as Fischer and Corcoran's (1994) *Measures for Clinical Practice* and Jordan and Franklin's (2004) *Clinical Assessment for Social Workers*. These usually can be found in your library's reference section. For additional suggestions for texts on existing scales, see Rubin and Babbie's (2005) *Research Methods for Social Work*.

If, on the other hand, you develop your own measurement instrument, allow time to share it with others and receive feedback.

(1)   What are the dependent variables (outcomes) you are considering?

(2)   Drawing from your literature review, how have others measured each outcome variable?

Specify each outcome variable, then complete the information requested in the following table. If the agency has measured these variables before, include those measures or questions here.

## Outcome Measures (Dependent Variables)

| | Article 1 | Article 2 |
|---|---|---|
| Author/Date | | |
| Measure | | |
| Description | | |
| Reliability/Validity | | |
| Who Collected, How Often, Time Involved | | |
| Sensitive to Change Over Short Period of Time? (Yes/No) | | |

(3)     Your intended measures:

    (a)     Circle those measures on the prior page that you plan to use. You may choose more than one. If you do not plan to use any of the measures, go to Part (b). Consider the time frame of your study. For which measures is it realistic to expect measurable change to occur within that time frame? Now, go to (d).


    (b)     If none of the above measures seems appropriate, or if you want to develop measures of your own in addition to conventional measures you have selected, indicate why.


    (c)     What measure(s) do you propose?

(d)    Evaluate whether the above measures have a cultural bias in terms of age; race; gender; social class; physical, mental or emotional ability; or sexual orientation. In the case of validated scales, with whom and with what age group have the scales been tested for validity and reliability?

(e)    Discuss potential limitations of your measures relative to reliability and validity.

Now you are ready to construct your research questionnaire and develop a plan administering it. Complete sections B, C, and D in Chapter 6, Survey Research.

# (C) Choosing a Design

Once you have specified your outcomes and measures, constructed your research instrument, and specified your plan for data collection, you are ready to choose your research design. The following questions will help you determine which design you will be able to use.

(1)     Can you *randomly assign* some participants to a group that will receive your intervention and others to either a group that will receive an alternative treatment (actually comparing the relative effectiveness of the two treatments) or to a waiting list group who will receive the treatment after the first group has finished the program?

If yes, then you can conduct a *control group design*, a true experimental design. Consult your research methods text for a review of that design. Proceed to (4).

If no, then proceed to the next question.

(2)     Is there a group that is similar to the group of individuals receiving your intervention? Can you gather the same information from this group over the same period of time as your treatment group?

If yes, then you can conduct a *comparison group design*, sometimes also called a *nonequivalent control group design*, a quasi-experimental design. Consult your research methods text for a review of that design. Proceed to (4).

If no, then proceed to the next question.

(3) If you cannot do either of the above, your last alternative is to conduct a *one group pretest-posttest design*. You will obtain baseline measures for participants prior to the intervention and then again at completion of the intervention. Consult your research methods text for a review of that design.

Keep in mind that a *one group pretest-posttest design* offers virtually no internal validity and thus does not provide evidence that the observed changes are a result of your intervention. *One group pretest-posttest designs* serve primarily for outcomes monitoring. Often, given the constraints of time and resources, this design is the only feasible one. It is of value nonetheless as it still requires completion of the tasks of specifying the link between intervention and objectives, developing outcome measures, and planning data collection procedures.

(4) Draw a diagram of your study design, using standard notation for group designs.

Your Design Type: _____

# (D) Threats to Internal Validity

Regardless of the design you have chosen, there will be limitations to your ability to demonstrate that the intervention is responsible for changes in your treatment group. These are known as threats to internal validity. Threats to internal validity are discussed in all research texts. Because students typically have difficulty applying these threats to particular studies, we present them below in lighter fashion. Some apply only to group designs rather than single-subject designs, so apply them to your study with consideration for your design type.

(1)     People dropping out of a study is a common and troublesome issue for researchers, so we ask you to address this threat specifically. Indicate your ideas for trying to reduce the number of *dropouts* in your study (referred to as attrition or experimental mortality).

        For the other threats listed below, indicate on a separate page each threat that is relevant to your study and your plans to address that threat. Depending on your design type, you may not be able to eliminate or reduce a potential threat, but you should at least recognize how it limits your conclusions.

# Threats to Internal Validity

### The Grandma Factor
- How do we know the changes we see are a result of our efforts and not Grandma's?
- This is known as the threat of **history:** extraneous events (potentially influential) that happen at the same time as treatment.

### Time Heals All Wounds
- How do we know the changes we see are a result of our efforts and not just the 6 month cycle of depression?
- How do we know the changes we see are a result of our efforts and not just the passage of time?
- This is known as the threat of **maturation** (and also, passage of time): changes over time that have nothing to do with the treatment, but nonetheless affect the results.

### Practice Makes Perfect
- How do we know the changes we see are a result of our efforts and not just a result of the fact that people got a chance to practice how to answer the questions (pretest)?
- How do we know the changes we see are a result of our efforts and not just a result of the fact that people know they are being observed or that they will be measured (reactivity effect)?
- This is known as a **testing** threat to internal validity: the effect a pretest has on how people do later on some posttest treatment measure.

### To Err Is Human
- How do we know the changes we see are a result of our efforts and not a result of poorly developed measures?
- How do we know the changes we see are a result of our efforts and not a function of using a different pretest and posttest that are not really equal or comparable?
- How do we know the changes we see are a result of our efforts and not a result of inconsistent ratings criteria from pretest to posttest or from one observer to another?
- This is known as an **instrumentation** threat: the effect of errors in measurement on our results.

# More Threats to Internal Validity

## *The Law of Averages*

- How do we know the changes we see are a result of our efforts and do not simply reflect the fact that we got most people on a really bad day, while they were at their worst?  Then at the posttest, when several of them were no longer at their worst, on average the group did better, but it had absolutely nothing to do with us.
- This is known as **statistical regression** (or regression to the mean): some change for the better will occur whenever we start with people at their worst, just because of the natural ebb and flow of struggles.

## *Choose Wisely*

- How do we know the changes we see are a result of our efforts and not a result of simply working with people who were highly motivated to change?
- How do we know the changes we see are a result of our efforts and not a result of who we studied?
- This threat is known as a **selection bias:** the extent to which a treatment group is not comparable to a nontreatment group.

## *Dropouts*

- How do we know the changes we see are a result of our efforts and not a function of the fact that everyone who did not benefit from our help, dropped out of the study, so our results are based only on those we did help?
- This threat to internal validity is known as **experimental mortality** or **attrition:** the rate at which people drop out of an intervention study before it is finished.

## *Copycat and Tattletale*

What about those times when we *don't* find our help to be beneficial—the ones we work with improve, but not any more than those we didn't work with? Could something else explain that?

- Maybe those we didn't work with got the same sort of help somewhere else; from copycats, so to speak.
- Maybe those we didn't work with are chums of those we did work with, and they got all our nuggets of wisdom from their buds; tattletales, so to speak.
- This threat is known as **imitation** (copycat) or **diffusion** (tattletale) of treatment — when groups to be compared really aren't so different relative to the services they are receiving.

# (E) Selecting a Sample and Assigning Groups

Students often confuse *random selection* (which has to do with *sample* selection) with *random assignment* (which has to do with how a treatment and control group are formed *after* a sample has been selected). That is why present it as *selecting* a sample and *assigning* groups.

Regardless of which design you are using, you must decide how you will select your sample of program participants. In some cases the number of program participants is small enough that you will choose to study all of them. This makes your study sample the same as your study population, the group to which you can generalize your study findings. In other cases, the number of program participants will be too large to include in your sample, and you will have to select some of them for your study. The larger group is the study *population* from which you select a study *sample*.

(1)    If you plan to conduct a *one group pretest-posttest design*, at this point you should complete Chapter 10, Sample Design.

If you plan to conduct a control group design, skip to (4).

(2)    If you plan to conduct a *comparison group design*, you will select two samples: those who receive the intervention and those who do not. The credibility of this design relies upon the extent to which you can demonstrate that your comparison group is similar to your treatment group.

For example, if you were to compare juvenile offenders receiving a therapeutic arts program to offenders in another facility without such a program, you would need to demonstrate that the groups were similar, but in what ways? To answer this question, you draw on your knowledge of the literature relative to the factors that have been shown to influence the outcomes you intend to measure.

In other words, if you found that the treatment group was better able to express anger appropriately at the end of the study as compared to the comparison group, you would not want someone to dispute your findings by noting that the comparison group was different to begin with. For example, if the juvenile offenders receiving treatment were at a minimum-security facility, and the juvenile offenders in the comparison group were at a maximum-security facility, one could argue that the reason the treatment group fared better on expressing anger appropriately was that they were a less violent group to begin with.

One resolution to this problem most often used by researchers is to use demographic characteristics as proxy measures for the comparability of the two groups. Because other characteristics are often linked to demographic differences, if you can demonstrate that your groups are similar in terms of demographics (age, race, gender, etc.), people will be willing to consider that other factors linked to your outcome are likely to be similar in the two groups.

Given these considerations, what populations do you think might provide an equivalent comparison group for your treatment group? List them below. Indicate how they are similar to and different from your treatment group.

(3)     Consider factors that might influence your program outcomes. List the factors that previous studies have shown to be related to the outcomes you are studying.

Would any of the groups you listed above *obviously* differ from your treatment group on any of these characteristics? If so, it is probably not a good choice. Consider, also, that whatever group becomes your comparison group, they will need to be available for data collection of the same type and at the same times as your treatment group.

Now you should complete Chapter 10, Sample Design once for your treatment group and a second time for your comparison group. Then turn to Part F in this chapter.

(4)     If you plan to conduct a control group design, you must randomly assign the individuals in your sample to separate groups, usually a group that receives the treatment you are studying and a group that receives either an alternative treatment or a group that is placed on a waiting list to receive services at a later date. The assumption of random assignment is that you will have created two groups whose participants are similar to each other on all characteristics. This assumption is easily violated in small samples.

For example, imagine a sample of 20 people randomly split into two groups. The assumption is that the numbers of males and females in one group will be the same in the other group, that the age groupings in one group will be the same as those in the other group, that the variation in attitudes in one group will be just the same in the other group, and so on. However, probability theory tells us that with only 20 people in our sample, it is quite possible that the two groups will not be entirely equivalent in these areas. Thus, it is necessary to gather and present basic demographic and baseline information about the two groups to consider the extent to which they are actually similar to each other.

More information on this idea of equivalency between groups is given in (2) above, and you are encouraged to read it now.

✓ On what variables can you compare your groups?

✓ Complete Chapter 10, Sample Design, then return to (C).

✓ Indicate whether you will use a wait list control group or alternative treatment control group.

✓ How will you randomly assign people to the two groups?

## (F) Write the METHODS Section

Again, this will be a first draft of this section because, as you proceed through the other steps, you may return and make revisions. This section will vary in length according to how many measures you have chosen. It should include (roughly one to two pages) the following information:

- Dependent variables (the target goals) and the client's input
- The chosen measure(s) for each variable and use in prior studies
- The validity and reliability of each measure
- The independent variable (the intervention)
- Indicate how groups were formed
- Details on the chosen design, rationale, and limitations
- Consent form and protection of data

## (G) Data Collection

Data collection should follow the plan you set out in this chapter. Once you have completed data collection, you will revise the methods section to report how you actually collected the data.

# Logic Model
# for the QUEST Program

**Program:**   QUEST
Provide bi-weekly telephone counseling to HIV+ individuals taking antiretroviral (ARV) medications.

**Objectives:**   (1) To improve adherence to medication.
(2) To improve physical health.

**Logic:**   Recent research on adherence to ARVs suggests that adherence rates greater than 90% are necessary to maintain suppression of HIV. Numerous studies have found that rates of adherence are generally low (40%-60%) because of the difficulty people have in adapting a complex medication regimen to their daily routine. If individuals can be helped to develop ways of adapting the medication regimen to their lifestyle rather than the other way around, and if they can be supported during the time required to develop a "habit of adherence," then adherence rates should improve.

**Design:**   Comparison group design:
$$\begin{array}{ccc} O_1 & X & O_2 \\ \hline O_3 & & O_4 \end{array}$$

**Samples:**   Experimental group:  25 randomly chosen patients from 217 outpatients at an HIV clinic at hospital X who are participants in the QUEST program.
Comparison group:  25 randomly chosen patients from 150 outpatients at an HIV clinic at hospital Y who are receiving standard case management services.
Experimental and comparison group are similar in that the clinics at both hospitals serve similar groups with respect to race, gender, and public vs. private pay.

**Hypotheses:**   (1)   At the end of three months, adherence will be higher for individuals who receive the intervention as compared to individuals in the comparison group.
(2)   At the end of three months physical health status will be better for individuals who receive the intervention as compared to individuals in the comparison group.

| Outcomes | Measures | Source of Data | When Collected | Where Collected | How Collected |
|---|---|---|---|---|---|
| Participants will demonstrate increases in adherence levels. | Number of doses taken as prescribed in each of past three days | Participant | Start of intervention (pretest) and end of intervention (posttest) | At home visit for pretest | Interview |
| | Number of pills left in prescription bottle on specific date compared to number that should be left | Pill count by interviewer | | At home visit for posttest | Interview |
| Participants will have better physical health. | Lab results: CD4 counts<br><br>Lab results: Viral load | Physician or Nurse (with signed consent) | Pretest and posttest | By mail | Questionnaire |

| Independent Variables | Measures | Source of Data | When Collected | Where Collected | How Collected |
|---|---|---|---|---|---|
| Intervention | Number of phone calls completed and home visits | Social workers | Bi-weekly | Office | Case records |
| Race | White (not Hispanic), Afr. Am., Hispanic or Latino, Asian, Amer. Ind., Other (specify) | Participant | Pretest | Home visit | Interview |
| Gender | Male, Female | Participant | Pretest | Home visit | Interview |
| Health Insurance | Private, Medicaid, Medicare, Ryan White Funds | Participant | Pretest and posttest | Home visit | Interview |
| Social Support | Number of persons living with participant | Participant | Pretest and posttest | Home visit | Interview |

# CHAPTER 10

# SAMPLE DESIGN

---

**Reminder:**

Review sample design in a methods text. Pay close attention to the difference between probability and nonprobability sampling methods. Within each of those two broad types of sampling methods, review the different types of samples that can be drawn.

---

The first thing you must decide is whether you will select a sample based on probability or nonprobability sampling methods. This decision is dependent on several factors, including how you plan to use the information you have collected and the constraints you will face in selecting a sample (accessibility of potential participants, time, and expense).

For example, if your ultimate goal is to use data collected from a sample to make statements about a larger group of people (as in some descriptive studies), probability sampling methods will be required. However, this goal will have to be balanced against the difficulty, time, and expense of drawing a probability sample from a well-defined population. If your ultimate goal is less concerned with the generalizability of your findings and more concerned with presenting detailed information about personal experiences (as in some exploratory studies) or evaluating a program or intervention (outcomes evaluation), then you may choose to select a nonprobability sample.

Probability samples are preferred for survey methods. Single-subject and outcomes evaluation typically use nonprobability samples because you are using the clients in your program and do not have a population from which to draw. Occasionally, you might be able to draw a probability sample from the clients served by the agency, in which case you should complete Part A.

If you are already certain about which type of sample you want to use, then proceed to Part A if you are going to do a probability sample, Part B if nonprobability. If you are uncertain about which type of sample would work best for your study, begin with Part A on probability samples. The questions should help you determine if a probability sample is feasible for your study.

# (A) For Probability Samples

(1)    What is the theoretical population for your study?

(2)    What will be your actual study population? Specify the criteria you will establish to determine if someone "fits" within your study population? Example: 1) at least 18 years of age, 2) with at least one child, and 3) a first time recipient of services at the agency. Be sure to specify the time frame (e.g., within the month of March).

(3)     Although the results from your sample are generalizable only to your study population, you are of course interested in adding to an understanding of the theoretical population. For example, since we can't study all the people who are homeless, we study some obtainable group of them, and what we learn is added to the body of knowledge about homeless people. We are thus required to discuss how our study population may differ from the theoretical population (only shelter users or only homeless people in small towns). This is helpful when trying to understand why findings from one study may differ from those of another.

In what ways will your study population differ from the theoretical population?

(4)     What will be the sampling frame (the actual list of potential participants) for your study population? Include either the actual size of the study population or provide your best estimate. Indicate any planned safeguards for obtaining confidential information.

You will probably need to explore this with your field instructor. In some instances you might need to know confidential information about people (diagnoses, problem situations) in order to determine their inclusion in the sampling frame—for example, a study of teens identified as alcohol or drug abusers in a child welfare agency that serves all categories of children. Generally in those situations, agency personnel must first obtain client permission before releasing names to you, even though you are in placement at the agency. This is especially true in large agencies that have several divisions.

Sometimes this ethical consideration is disregarded, and it is your responsibility as an ethical researcher to ensure attention to it. To help you consider how important it is to have client consent for release of information, consider how you would feel if someone was giving to others, without your permission or knowledge, information about you, one of your children, or your parent.

(5)     Consider any possible biases in your sampling frame—for example, omitted names, organization by single-service users versus multiple-service users, organization by length of service, court referral versus self-referral, repeat listings of the same name, listings by family members. List those biases below and how you either will be able to correct for them or will need to include them in a discussion of your sample's limitations.

(6)     What specific type of probability sample will you choose (simple random, systematic)? Include your rationale, and consider stratification prior to systematic sampling as a means of enhancing the representativeness of your sample. For stratification, on what variable(s) (sample member characteristics) would you stratify and why?

(7)   Indicate the specific procedure for sample selection. Indicate who will screen potential sample members and how they will do it.

(8)   When you ask people to participate, some will refuse. You should keep a tally of how many refuse so that you can calculate and report a participation rate. Also, it is helpful later, when considering possible biases of your sample, to compare participants with those who refused to participate. What information could you collect about nonparticipants (from observation, screening questions) that would enable you to make comparisons?

(9)    What size will your sample be? Indicate your rationale and
       discuss the feasibility of your sample size relative to time;
       expense; means of contact; and level of difficulty in contact,
       screening, and selection.

(10)   Pay close attention to the inclusion and representation of people
       of color, a group frequently underrepresented in research
       studies. If you intend to make statements about people of color,
       how have you ensured that people of color will be included in
       your sample in sufficient numbers to provide meaningful data
       about them? (Do NOT report results where you pool several
       racial or ethnic groups into a category labeled "other." It is
       disrespectful and provides no useful information.)

(11)   In summary, state clearly to whom you expect to be able to generalize your findings, based on the sampling plan you have devised.

(12)   Discuss the strengths and limitations of your sample design—for example, the type of sample and its weaknesses, the size of your sample, and its generalizability.

## (B) For Nonprobability Samples
### (typically used in outcomes evaluation and qualitative studies)

(1) What is your specific group of interest?

(2) What are the possible sources that you have considered for obtaining sample members and the pros and cons of each?

(3)    What are the screening and selection criteria for your sample?

Indicate the specific procedure for sample selection. Indicate who will screen potential sample members and how they will do it.

You will probably need to explore this with your field instructor. In some instances you might need to know confidential information about people (diagnoses, problem situations) in order to determine their potential inclusion in your sample—for example, a study of teens identified as alcohol or drug abusers in a child welfare agency that serves all categories of children. Generally in those situations, agency personnel must first obtain client permission before releasing names to you, even though you are in placement at the agency. This is especially true in large agencies that have several divisions.

Sometimes this ethical consideration is disregarded, and it is your responsibility as an ethical researcher to ensure attention to it. To help you consider how important it is to have client consent for release, consider how you would feel if someone was giving to others that particular information about you or one of your children.

Indicate any planned safeguards for obtaining confidential information.

(4)     What specific type of sample will you draw?

(5)     What size will your sample be? Indicate your rationale and discuss the feasibility of your sample size relative to time; expense; means of contact; and level of difficulty in contact, screening, and selection.

(6)   Pay close attention to the inclusion of people of color, a group frequently overlooked in research studies. Indicate below how you will ensure that your study will represent people of color. (Do NOT report results where you pool several racial or ethnic groups into a category labeled "other." It is disrespectful and provides no useful information.)

(7)   Discuss the strengths and limitations of your sample design. Because experiences vary across cultures, how will you ensure that your study will reflect those differences?

## (C) Write the SAMPLE Section

This first draft will be approximately two pages and should cover the details of your sampling design. Later, after you have collected your data, you will add how your sampling procedures actually occurred, including participation rate and the demographic characteristics of your sample members.

If possible, you should compare participants to nonparticipants on any information you may have for both groups (age, race, gender, or social class) to provide information about the extent to which participants are similar to, or different from, nonparticipants.

# CHAPTER 11

# PROTECTION OF RESEARCH PARTICIPANTS

**Reminder:**
Review your text on the protection of research participants and constructing consent forms.

Earlier you discovered the procedures of the university and agency for protecting research participants and obtaining approval of research studies. Review boards typically require information about the proposed data collection procedures, sample selection, and informed consent, as well as copies of data collection instruments, including interview agenda. You have developed this information in earlier chapters of the workbook. Complete the following sections, putting the information into the required format.

Research participants must be provided with information about the study and how it might affect them. A parent or guardian can act on behalf of participants who cannot understand or consent for themselves. With few exceptions, parental consent is required for participants who are under age 18.

When using innocuous and anonymous questionnaires in survey research, a consent form may not be required; however, you have an ethical obligation to provide information about the study to the participants. This is usually done in a cover letter accompanying the survey or questionnaire. Check with your university's IRB for clarification.

Social workers have additional obligations relative to the ethical conduct of research. If you become aware that someone is being abused or might harm him or herself or another person, you are obligated to report it to the appropriate agency or authority. If you anticipate situations where this might be revealed, you should include in your consent form that you have a legal responsibility to report these incidents and would be obligated to violate the participant's confidentiality relative to that issue.

# (A) Construct a Consent Form

## Reminder:
IRB and agency approval must be obtained
before collecting data!

(1) Use the guidelines provided by the university IRB for what to include in the consent form. Although we have included samples of consent forms in this chapter on pages 165-166, be sure to check with your university's IRB. We recommend that you also ask for sample consent forms from the university IRB or your course instructor. Your methods text will also give information about constructing consent forms. You will submit the consent form along with your packet of information to the IRB. Remember, if you are including persons under age 18 and their parent or guardian, you may need two different consent forms, one for each group.

On separate pages, list each point or item you must include in your consent form according to the university IRB and agency requirements.

(2) On a separate page, prepare a draft of the consent form. Obtain feedback from your course instructor and agency instructor. Revise and finalize the consent form.

## (B) Outline Procedures for Obtaining Informed Consent

Indicate how you plan to inform participants about the study and obtain their consent to participate. Include specific procedures for children or youth under age 18 if applicable.

Please note that young children are usually asked orally for their assent to participate in a study. If young children are participating in your study, indicate how you will obtain assent from them. Include the script you will use for obtaining assent.

# (C) Confidentiality Safeguards

(1)    Describe how you will protect the privacy and confidentiality of the research participants at the time you collect the data.

(2)    Describe your plans for storage and protection of data, including the signed consent forms. Also, indicate a date at which point your data will be destroyed. We recommend you include this information in your consent form.

(3)   Describe your plans for protecting privacy and confidentiality in your presentation of findings and written report.

# (D) Request Agency Approval

Indicate the steps you have taken for agency approval of your study. (The agency may or may not have a specific process for approval of research. If there is no agency process in place, we encourage you to obtain written permission to carry out the study from the director of the agency.)

## (E) Request IRB Approval

(1)   Using what you have written in the workbook, prepare the information requested by the university and agency IRBs.

## Sample Informed Consent Form

We would like you to participate in the Evaluation of *[program name]*. Your participation is important to us and will help us assess the effectiveness of the program. As a participant in *[program name]* we will ask you to *[complete a questionnaire, answer questions in an interview, or other task]*.

We will keep all of your answers confidential. Your name will never be included in any reports and none of your answers will be linked to you in any way. The information that you provide will be combined with information from everyone else participating in the study.

*[If information/data collection includes questions relevant to behaviors such as child abuse, drug abuse, or suicidal behaviors, the program should make clear its potential legal obligation to report this information—and that confidentiality may be broken in these cases. Make sure that you know what your legal reporting requirements are before you begin your evaluation.]*

You do not have to participate in the evaluation. Even if you agree to participate now, you may stop participating at any time or refuse to answer any question. Refusing to be part of the evaluation will not affect your participation or the services you receive in *[program name]*.

If you have any questions about the study you may call *[name and telephone number of evaluator, program manager, or community advocate]*.

By signing below, you confirm that this form has been explained to you and that you understand it.

**Please Check One:**
❑   AGREE TO PARTICIPATE
❑   DO NOT AGREE TO PARTICIPATE


_____Signed
Participant or Parent/Guardian

_____Date

From: United State Department of Health and Human Services. (1997). *The Program Manager's Guide to Evaluation*, p. 77.

## Informed Consent to Participate in a Study of the Crisis Program at Huckleberry House Youth Services

1.  **Why is the study being conducted?** Huckleberry House is conducting a study to find out if the agency's crisis program is helpful to families. You have been asked to take part because you have used these services.

2.  **What are you being asked to do?** You will be one of about 25 youth who are interviewed about their experience with the program and program staff. You will be asked some questions about what brought you to the program and what problems you and your parent(s) have been experiencing. We will contact you three months from now to see if things have changed for you. The interview usually takes about 30 minutes. Your first interview will be on the premises of Huckleberry House. Your second interview in three months will be by telephone.

3.  **Is this voluntary?** Yes. You are under no obligation to participate. If you agree to participate, you can ask the interviewer to skip any questions that you'd rather not answer. Also, you are free to stop the interview at any time. You are also free to decline to participate in the follow-up interview.

4.  **What are the advantages of participating?** Participating in this study will help Huckleberry House improve its services to youth and their families.

5.  **Will participating in this study affect the services you are receiving?** No. Whether or not you agree to participate in the study will not affect the type or amount of services you are eligible to receive.

6.  **Is this confidential?** Yes. Nothing learned about you by the researchers will be told to anyone else. The study staff will remove identifying information from your completed questionnaire. All records will be identified only by a number, and the link between that number and your name will be kept in a locked file that is available only to the researchers, not to Huckleberry House program staff. Once the study is completed, all records of your name will be destroyed. All data will be kept in locked files. Everything that you say is strictly confidential, and any reports or other published data based on this study will appear only in the form of summary statistics without names or other identifying information.

7.  **What risks do you face if you participate?** There are no risks expected if you answer the questions.

8.  **Who do you contact if you have questions about this research?** If you have any questions about the study, you can ask your interviewer or call the agency director, _____, at _____ or the faculty supervisor of this project, _____ at _____.

AI. Your signature below indicates that you consent to be interviewed, that you have been given a copy of this consent form, and that you have read and understood it.

Signature:_____ Date:_____

A2.Witnessed by:

Signature:_____ Date:_____

# CHAPTER 12

# DATA ANALYSIS FOR SURVEYS AND OUTCOMES EVALUATION

This chapter of the workbook is divided into five sections: (A) presentation of descriptive information, (B) statistical tests for descriptive data, (C) presentation of group comparisons, (D) statistical tests for group comparisons, and (E) testing the relationship between continuous variables. The data analysis we cover here is similar for surveys, outcomes evaluations, and data that someone else has collected (referred to as analysis of existing data).

In this chapter, we introduce only the most commonly used bivariate statistical tests: chi-square (from cross tabulation tables), t-test (two groups), ANOVA (for multiple groups), and correlation (for two continuous variables). Our presentation of the bivariate tests assumes you have had prior instruction on them and understand which tests are appropriate to use. Remember that bivariate analyses are only suggestive of relationships, not definitive; multivariate analyses may reveal more complex relationships among several variables. For more complex analyses or those involving sample sizes less than 20, we recommend that you consult other sources. We suggest Weinbach and Grinnell's (2004) *Statistics for Social Workers* or Green and Salkind's (2005) *Using SPSS for Windows* for helpful information on statistical analysis.

## A Word for the Statistically Intimidated

Many people are intimidated by statistics. Too often they believe that "only people who are good in math can understand statistics." This belief leads them to assume they cannot do any analysis involving statistics. This is simply not true. If you consider yourself statistically challenged, in this short section, we will help you to learn that you can do basic, useful statistical analysis for your study. You may not be able to complete a regression analysis. That's okay. You can find someone with more training than you who can do it for you—much as you might consult with a social worker with more training than you on how to handle a difficult client situation. It is to your advantage to have a general understanding of the procedure, but you don't have to know everything about statistics. You certainly can complete the other less complex statistical procedures (e.g., t-tests, cross-tabulations) yourself.

## A Word on Statistical Analysis

Statistical tests make it possible for you to generalize from a sample to the larger population from which it was drawn. If you conducted a survey of 100 randomly chosen clients at a clinic and asked how many ever had an HIV test, your sample finding would be your best estimate of the testing rate among all clients of that clinic. From this estimate, researchers create a range (confidence interval) around that estimate. This is the range within which we expect to find the actual value of the population.

Statistical tests allow you to determine how likely it is that your findings are due to chance. This is commonly referred to as *statistical significance.* If it is likely that your findings can be attributed to chance, then you cannot conclude that you have found a difference between groups or a relationship between variables. For example, looking at Table 1 on page 175, our findings show that a higher percentage of Whites return to the Kansas City Free Health Clinic for their HIV test results than do African Americans or Hispanics. Is this a finding that we can attribute to the relationship between race and returning for results? Or is it merely due to chance and not likely to be found in another sample of HIV testers? If we find statistical significance, we conclude that our finding is *not* due to chance, and we may decide to develop an intervention to increase the rate at which African Americans and Hispanics return for their HIV test results.

Statistical testing, then, allows us to rule out chance as a possible explanation for the result we found. This is why researchers emphasize using strong sample designs. Probability sampling, an assumption for most statistical tests, is a process of selecting a group of people from a population in such a way as to best represent the population. How well was that accomplished? With statistical testing you can calculate a measure of how much error there is in using the sample's findings to generalize to the population (that's where margin of error comes into play).

In conducting a statistical test you are actually converting your findings into a standardized value that results in a test statistic (e.g., t = 2.3). Then that standardized value is used to determine the probability (p-value) that the findings are reflective of a pattern in the population, i.e., can be generalized to the population or are simply due to chance. If the findings are probably due to chance, we cannot generalize the findings to the population.

Computer analysis gives you the test statistic and the p-value that is associated with it. The p-value is what you are interested in. A low probability (low p-value, usually .05 or less) means that getting this finding by chance is low. We can conclude that our sample finding most likely (not definitively as there are no certainties in behavioral research) reflects what is actually happening in the population. In other words, we can generalize our findings to the larger population. In Table 1 on page 175, the probability of getting the differences among the three racial groups simply by chance, was quite low, p = .003. Therefore, we can generalize the findings from our sample to the population of all clients at the clinic.

How low is low? Five percent (.05) or less is generally accepted as the standard in social science research. So if our sample finding could occur by chance less than 5 out of 100 times (p = .05), we conclude that the finding is statistically significant.

This is the key to understanding statistical analysis. Remember that all statistical tests are tests of the probability that the findings can be attributed to chance.

## Types of Statistical Tests

There are basically three groups of statistics: univariate (one variable), bivariate (two variables), and multivariate (three or more variables). Bivariate and multivariate analyses use various statistical tests, each designed to answer the same question: How big is big? That is, how big must the difference between groups be? Or how big must the relationship between variables be, in order to be statistically significant rather than due to chance? When we say the results are statistically significant, we are saying our observations in the sample can be generalized to the population.

## Computerized Analysis

First decide whether you will do hand tabulation or computer data entry and analysis. The advantages of the latter should be obvious, but you may not have computer expertise and the ability to conduct statistical analysis on a computer. We suggest that you check with your course instructor or staff at your agency who may be able to help you with computer analysis. If, however, you do hand tabulations, we do not recommend doing statistical analysis beyond presenting basic descriptive information.

Any number of statistical programs are available, including programs for advanced statistical analysis—such as SPSS© and SAS©. These are not difficult to learn but do require some effort. Spreadsheet programs you may already know—such as Excel©—also allow for basic statistical analysis. We will not cover the technical aspects of computer analysis (data file development and statistical programming).

## Table Construction

Keep in mind that there is not one "correct" table format for the presentation of your results. The APA Style Manual provides guidance for constructing and presenting tables in a manuscript. You can also look through the articles you used for your literature review for help with designing tables. Present your findings simply and clearly so they are easy to understand.

# (A) Presentation of Descriptive Information

For the steps below, begin by drafting tables for your variables. Do not put values in the tables yet. As you work through the steps, you will develop several ideas about the best way to present your data and how you want your final tables to look. When you have decided the best format, then complete the tables with the data findings.

(1)     Frequency Distributions:

The most basic level of analysis involves calculating how many people gave a certain response to each question in the interview or questionnaire or are in certain categories. These are called frequency distributions. You may group some categories of responses together rather than report a long series of responses. For example, rather than report how many people were of every age between 20 and 89, you can group categories together into intervals such as, 20-29, 30-39, etc. Then, report the number of participants in each grouped interval. Consult a text for assistance in constructing intervals.

For continuous variables you may also report, or only report, the means of variables and other associated statistics that will be discussed in the next section. You may choose to display some of your findings in graph form (bar, line, or pie chart). Make your choices based on what makes the presentation of findings easy for your audience to understand. Refer to a research text for how to construct various graphs.

On a separate sheet, list all of the variables in your study. Mark those variables that you think would be best presented with a graph (bar, line, or pie chart) instead of a table. Sketch the types of graphs you plan to use.

(2)     Means, Medians, and Standard Deviations:

Reporting the mean (commonly referred to as the average) requires that the variables are continuous (such as age, income, etc.) rather than discrete (gender, race, religion, etc.). Remember to consult a research methods or statistics text for appropriate statistics to use in your study.

You might be interested in knowing the mean of all the responses to a particular question, e.g., the average age of the participants in your study. Knowing the median (middle) value of the variables is also informative, especially when there are one or two extremely high or low scores, which tend to create a misleading mean. Median values can also be calculated by hand or by computer.

If you are using a computer for data analysis, you can easily calculate and report the standard deviations for your continuous variables. Remember, the standard deviation shows the dispersion of the data—how the scores are distributed around the mean. A high standard deviation alerts us that there is a large amount of variation between the mean and individual scores in the sample.

In your list of study variables determine those that are continuous and calculate the mean, median, and standard deviation.

(3)     Decide which descriptive statistics to present in your report and the order in which you will present them. Often, more than one table is helpful. For example, one table may present the demographic characteristics of the sample and another may present frequencies of the key variables in your study. Begin with general information and move to specific findings that answer your research question

To help organize your presentation of descriptive findings make two lists: primary findings and secondary findings. The primary findings should relate directly to your research question and should be given the most attention in your narrative and visual presentations.

Organize your primary and secondary findings below sketching out mock tables and graphs. Then complete the tables with the results from your sample.

# (B) Statistical Tests for Descriptive Data

(1)   Make a list of the descriptive findings you want to generalize to the population (e.g., mean age, percent using services, percent following through with a referral, mean sessions attended). Indicate whether each variable is continuous or discrete.

(2)   Using a statistical program, for each variable construct a 95% confidence interval around the sample estimate. For continuous variables you will use the standard error of the mean. For discrete variables you will use the margin of error.

(3)   Create the table you will use to present these data. In many cases you will simply add this information to the tables you created in section A.

# (C) Presentation of Group Comparisons

Generally, people are interested in comparing different groups of people on certain characteristics. Group comparisons are bivariate (two variable) analyses. They are used to provide additional information about the sample separated into groups. For example, in a needs assessment, you may be interested in comparing the identified needs (variable 1) reported by men versus women (variable 2). Or you might want to compare the number of sessions attended (variable 1) for two different groups of participants—self-referred individuals and court-referred individuals (variable 2). Group comparisons provide that information. Table 1 below shows an example of how descriptive data might be broken down by racial group and presented for a sample of clients who were tested for HIV at a clinic.

Table 1
*Returned for HIV Test Results and HIV Risk Level by Racial Group*

|  | Race | | |
|  | African American n = 63 | Hispanic n = 14 | White n = 121 |
|---|---|---|---|
| Returned for HIV test result [a] | 76.2% n = 48 | 85.7% n = 12 | 93.4% n = 113 |
| Risk level [b] (1-low to 10-high) |  |  |  |
| Mean | 2.0 | 2.5 | 3.3 |
| Standard Deviation | 2.7 | 4.4 | 6.3 |
| Median | 2 | 2 | 3 |

[a] Chi-Square = 11.5, p = .003
[b] F (ANOVA) = 1.27, p = .282

Table 2 below shows an example of comparing participant outcomes (attended all classes and number of incidents) in two programs, a Therapeutic Arts Program and a Recreational Program.

Table 2
*Attended all Classes and Number of Incidents by Group Assignment*

|  | Group | |
|---|---|---|
|  | Therapeutic Arts Program n = 22 | Recreational Program n = 26 |
| Attended all classes | 68% n = 15 | 73% n = 19 |
| Number of incidents |  |  |
| Mean | 4.0 | 4.2 |
| Standard Deviation | 5.5 | 4.5 |
| Median | 3 | 3 |

[a] Chi-Square = .138, p = .758
[b] t = -.107, p = .916

(1)    List on a separate page in columns the groups you would like to compare. In rows to the left of the columns list the variables on which you would like to compare the groups. You can either do the calculations yourself by hand or give this list to a computer programmer for calculations.

(2)    For each group, calculate the descriptive statistics—for example, the frequency, mean, standard deviation, percentage and number, or median—of the responses to each variable of interest. Enter them in the appropriate cells in tables on a separate sheet.

We provide mock tables below as models for you to use. Although these are developed for program outcome studies, they can be used for any group comparisons (male versus female, service users versus non-users, etc.)

Be sure to include the sample size (n) and group size (n), and also the group percentages for comparison purposes. Examine your APA Style Manual for how to format tables in your manuscript. Empirical articles will also have tables that can help you construct your tables.

Table number
*Table name*

| | Groups | |
|---|---|---|
| | Treatment Group (n = ) | Control or Comparison Group (n = ) |
| Measure at Pretest | % <br> n = | % <br> n = |
| Mean <br> Standard Deviation | | |
| Measure at Posttest | % <br> n = | % <br> n = |
| Mean <br> Standard Deviation | | |

$\chi^2 =$ , $p =$ .

The table below shows how you can present data for two groups compared on dichotomous measures—for example, outcomes at posttest for a treatment and control or comparison group.

Table number
*Table name*

| | Groups | |
| --- | --- | --- |
| | Treatment Group (n =  ) | Control or Comparison Group (n =  ) |
| Achieved | % <br> n = | % <br> n = |
| Not Achieved | % <br> n = | % <br> n = |

$\chi^2 =$     , p =     .

# (D) Statistical Tests for Group Comparisons

(1) Now complete the appropriate statistical test for each group comparison.

    (a)    When the outcome measure is discrete:

            Conduct a chi-square statistical test of the differences between the two groups.

    (b)    When the outcome measure is continuous:

            Conduct an independent groups t-test of the differences between the two group means.

(2)     For one group pretest-posttest design:

In the case of only one group, the same logic as above applies, but different tests are used.

(a)     When the outcome measure is discrete:

While similar to a cross tabulation, in this instance there is no grouping variable since there is only one group. The two variables are the dichotomous (yes or no) measures at pretest and posttest.

Complete the table below presenting your outcome results. Include the McNemar significance test (one of the nonparametric tests). Look for examples in your empirical articles.

Table Number

_____
                          Table Name
_____

|  | Dichotomous Outcome Measure at Posttest (n= ) | |
|---|---|---|
| Dichotomous Outcome Measure at Pretest (n = ) | Yes n = | No n = |
| Yes n = | | |
| No n = | | |
| McNemar = , p = . | | |

(b)     When the outcome measure is continuous:

To statistically examine the change for participants from baseline (when pretest measures were taken) to the end of the intervention (when posttest measures are taken) *in one group*, you must conduct a dependent groups t-test (also referred to as a correlated groups t-test, a paired groups t-test, or matched groups t-test). This allows you to determine whether any change in the outcome measure from pre- to posttest is big enough to suggest the change was not due to chance. Rather, it would indicate change that is statistically significant rather than just due to chance.

Table Number
*Table Name*

| | Outcome Measure |
|---|---|
| Pretest | $n =$ |
|     Mean | |
|     Standard Deviation | |
| | |
| Posttest | $n =$ |
|     Mean | |
|     Standard Deviation | |

$t =$     , $p =$     .

## (E) Testing the Relationship between Continuous Variables

In some instances, you may wish to compare two variables that are both continuous. For example, in an HIV clinic study, the staff were interested in how a person's self-appraisal of HIV risk was related to (1) the number of sexual partners he or she had indicated and (2) the person's age. Using a Pearson correlation coefficient, they reported:

Table 3
*Correlations between*
*HIV Risk and Selected Characteristics*

| | |
|---|---|
| Number of sex partners in past 12 months | .28* |
| Age | .14 |

*$p < .01$

Create a table below presenting your outcome results.

Table Number
*Table Name*

Variable 1

Variable 2

*$p =$

Be sure and have someone review your tables for clarity and accuracy.

# CHAPTER 13

# DATA ANALYSIS FOR QUALITATIVE RESEARCH

**Reminder:**
Review a text specifically devoted to qualitative methods. A general research text may not provide enough information for you to conduct a good qualitative analysis.

Recall that the goal of qualitative research is to provide an in-depth understanding of a phenomenon from the perspective of the research participants. Strategies for qualitative analysis vary and can be quite complicated. Keep in mind that you want to present the words and experiences of the research participants.

Your aim as a novice researcher is to conduct an analysis that organizes and summarizes the textual accounts of your participants and incorporates your observations. Your task is to identify themes and patterns in the data and offer interpretations of them. First, you will reduce the pages of data, your notes and observations, to a summarization of common topics and themes that participants have presented, with the goal of answering your research question. Next, you will organize the topics and themes, and select some representative quotes to illustrate your main points. Finally, you will offer your interpretation of the findings and your explanation for similarities and differences in, or exceptions to, the findings.

Because methods of qualitative analysis are less clear-cut than methods for quantitative analysis, we recommend that you specify as clearly and accurately as possible how you will conduct the analysis.

We strongly suggest that you type the data (either in its entirety or, at a minimum, the portions of the interviews that address your research topic) into a computer for analysis.

Software programs, such as The Ethnograph and HyperRESEARCH, can assist with qualitative analysis. These programs help *manage* the data, but you must be able to *do the interpretation* that is crucial to qualitative analysis. The steps we suggest for qualitative analysis do not require a software program. You will be able to conduct your analysis using a word processor.

# (A) First Level Coding

(1)   Read through all the data—the interviews, your notes, and any other sources of data you have. As you read through your data several times, identify the common topics that participants discuss. Keep a list of all the topics you identify. Also, take notes (called analytical memos) of your thoughts and observations as you read the data. Read through the data until you cannot identify any new topics.

List your topics here.

(2)    For each topic you listed, identify the excerpts (often referred to as meaning units) of data that relate to them by highlighting the relevant text. Excerpts are sections of each participant's responses that relate to each of your topics. Your task is to determine how much of the participant's comments are related to each topic. Your excerpts can range in length from a portion of a sentence to several paragraphs or pages, depending on how much the participant has said related to the topic.

Here is where a word processor is invaluable. You can easily block, move, and copy excerpts into topic files.

(3)    Sort and organize the data by placing the excerpts into the topic areas you have identified. This step is commonly called *first level coding.* As you read, you will *constantly compare* each excerpt to the others. Excerpts with similar meanings will be placed in the same topic area and given the same code.

Codes are basically short-hand notations for your topic areas. For example, if you are coding "participants responses related to positive interactions with social workers" you might assign a code POS SW to all the excerpts in which participants discuss that topic.

Excerpts that are different will be assigned to different codes. Some excerpts may fit into more than one topic and therefore have more than one code. Throughout the process, you will reorder and refine your topics into categories of broader groupings of topics. You may identify new topics that you had not previously thought of. Add them to your list of categories.

## (B) Second Level Coding

Second level coding involves a deeper level of analysis and interpretation of the data. In first level coding, you placed similar excerpts from each participant together and assigned them a specific code. You also grouped the topic areas that related to each other into broader categories.

Now your task is to examine all excerpts with the same code to compare excerpts across individual participants. Read what all the participants said, all the excerpts, for each topic area. As you read, identify themes within the topic areas that are illustrated across the participants' responses. Ask yourself:

✓   What are the main themes that are important to answering my research question?

✓   What similarities and differences do I see in the responses?

✓   Are there any relationships, trends, or patterns across responses?

✓   Are there exceptions to the themes I have identified?


(1) List your themes here:

(2)    Now arrange themes you have identified to answer research questions. Be sure to include each participant's voice in your presentation.

    ✓  Which themes seem to belong together?

    ✓  What order of presentation of themes makes sense?

List your revised themes here:

# (C) Select Excerpts to Represent Each Theme

(1)    Select representative excerpts and anecdotal accounts for each theme. Provide one or two excerpts to include in the results section of your paper so that the reader can "see" how you arrive at your findings.

On separate pages, compile the representative excerpts that you will include in your final paper.

# (D) Obtain Feedback from Research Participants

(1)     This important step in qualitative research will add credibility to
your findings. If possible obtain feedback from your research
participants regarding the categories, themes, trends, and
patterns you identified. Ask participants if they support or
disagree with your findings and conclusions. Write their
feedback on separate pages and include their feedback in your
final report.

(2)     Another way to establish credibility in your study is to carefully
and thoroughly document what you have done and how you
have done it. Include this information in your final report. It will
clarify the choices you have made, and why, for the reader.

# (E)  Relate Your Findings to the Literature

(1)     Finally, return to the literature to explore the concepts and ideas
that emerged from your study. Identify themes and relationships
that others have found and report them in your final report.

## Caution:
You are reporting findings based on the people in your study
only. You must be careful to avoid using findings to generalize
to others. Rather, your study is exploratory and offers tentative
suggestions that require further study. For a discussion of
trustworthiness, credibility, dependability, and generalization,
review a qualitative methods text.

# CHAPTER 14

# DATA ANALYSIS FOR SINGLE-SUBJECT DESIGN RESEARCH

**Reminder:**

Refer to a research text for ways to construct, analyze, and interpret graphed results of single-subject design studies.

The significance of your single-subject study findings should be evaluated in each of three ways: visual significance, statistical significance, and substantive (clinical) significance.

## (A) Visual Significance

The first analysis, visual significance, is the primary way you will have used your study results with your client. The researcher as practitioner and the client share constant feedback during the intervention phase. You can review the results with the client by using the graphed data, allowing both to visualize the progress of their work together.

Visual significance is inherently a subjective assessment of your findings. Essentially, it asks you and the client to examine the graphed results and determine from your points of view whether the intervention was successful.

On a separate sheet draw a graph of your findings with the X- and Y-axes clearly marked, as well as all baseline and intervention phases. Connect the plotted points on the graph, and comment below on the visual significance of your findings.

189

(1)     What changes in the target goal do you observe? What is the trend at baseline and at intervention?

(2)     Are there any abrupt or unusual changes that warrant explanation (e.g., number of temper tantrums, spikes on a certain day, or for one day only there are none)?

(3)     Does it appear that the intervention was effective, ineffective, or unclear? Support your answer.

# (B) Statistical Significance

Determining statistical significance is a more objective way of evaluating your findings. It relies on the principles of probability theory to rule out chance fluctuations in your data as a possible explanation for your findings.

There are three procedures available for determining statistical significance in single-subject studies. Refer to a text, and seek your instructor's assistance as you choose one of the following methods: celeration line, two standard deviation procedure, proportion/frequency procedure.

Complete one test, detailing how it was done and the final results.

# (C) Substantive or Clinical Significance

What we mean by substantive or clinical significance is analysis of whether the results of the intervention met the expectations of both the practitioner and the client. Regardless of whether the results were statistically significant, does the client and/or the worker feel the client has made substantial progress? Is the client functioning significantly better now than when you began your work together? Substantive significance asks each person to step back from the work they have done and assess it from their own experience and perspective.

Comment below on the clinical significance of your findings. Also ask your client to comment on your work together and the graphed findings. Include your client's comments here.

# CHAPTER 15

# WRITING THE FINAL REPORT

---

**Reminder:**

Allow enough time to write your research report. Having completed each chapter of the workbook, you have a rough draft of your paper. We recommend that you follow the outline at the end of this chapter and write a second draft to share with your field instructor, agency staff, and peers for feedback and comments. You may also seek help from your school's writing center.

---

This chapter focuses on presenting your findings in a written research paper. Basically, your report will include what you did and why, what you found, and what it means. Your research paper will expand on earlier chapters and include new sections on findings and discussion. From this paper, you can develop a presentation for your agency, for your peers in field placement, or for participants at a conference. If you are interested in submitting your study for publication, check with your course instructor for guidance.

Refer to the Research Paper Outline at the end of this chapter.

# (A) Rewrite Earlier Sections of Your Paper

Revise earlier drafts of the Introduction, Literature Review, and Methods sections, changing the tense from future (you will study) to past (you studied). Incorporate the feedback you received from your course instructor, field instructor, and others along the way.

# (B) For the SAMPLE Section

Revise your draft of Chapter 10 and include the results of your sampling procedures.

(1)   Describe the criteria and procedures for sample selection as they were carried out in your study.

(2)   Present the results of the sampling procedures, the response rate, and demographic characteristics of the sample members.

(3)   Depending on how you selected your sample, compare participants to those who refused to participate.

# (C) Write the FINDINGS Section

Drawing from earlier chapters of the workbook to guide you through data analysis, organize and present the findings of your study.

(1)   In narrative form, present your primary and secondary findings.

(2)   Visually and textually display data that will help the reader understand your findings.

    (a)   When appropriate, display data in tables, graphs, or charts.

    (b)   Write the narrative section to describe visual displays.

    (c)   For qualitative studies, you will use excerpts identified in Chapter 12 to illustrate themes.

(3)   Review the findings section of your report to be sure that you present the *results* of your study, not your interpretation of them.

# (D) Write the DISCUSSION Section

Refer to the Research Paper Outline for the topics to be included. Use the following questions to list the main points to be included in this section. After you have answered each question, write the full draft of the discussion section.

(1)   Discuss your interpretation of the findings:

    (a)   Refer to your original research question and discuss what you learned about it.

    (b)   Refer to the literature you reviewed and comment on how your findings relate to that literature.

(2)    Develop implications for social work:

What do the findings of your study mean for the agency, staff members, the participants, and/or the social work profession?


(3)    Provide recommendations for social workers:

Based on your study, what policies, programs, and/or practice actions do you think should be taken by your agency or social work practitioners?


(4)    Report the limitations of your study relative to measures, data collection procedures, and sample design.


(5)    Make suggestions for future research:

What else do we need to know that would help us better serve our clients? What would you recommend to the next researcher who wants to study this topic? What other questions evolved from this study? List questions that emerged from your study that you think future research should address.


# (E)  Compile the REFERENCES

Include all the sources of information (journal articles, books, and reports) that you used in writing your report. Consult a style manual for proper form.

# (F) Compile the APPENDICES

Include a copy of the consent form and your research instrument or interview agenda.

# (G) Write the ABSTRACT

An abstract is a brief overview summary of your study and results, usually 100 words or less. Write the abstract and place it immediately following your title page.

Here are two examples of an abstract written for the same study.

## ABSTRACT EXAMPLE 1

Objectives: We sought to convey patient experiences with adherence to antiretroviral therapy.

Methods: We conducted three focus groups lasting two hours each with a total of 21 men, utilizing a semi-structured interview guide.

Results: Participants discussed their desire for information, the importance of the relationship with care providers, the impact of medication side effects, the role of social supports, and the responsibility of self as factors influencing adherence. Self-efficacy, the curvilinear relationship between adherence and severity of illness.

Conclusions: Social workers should educate themselves about antiretroviral regimens and side effects; help individuals gain access to information; facilitate relationships and enhance communication between patient and providers; start support groups or refer individuals to existing support groups.

## ABSTRACT EXAMPLE 2

People who are HIV positive and people who have been diagnosed with AIDS have new hope in the form of antiretroviral medications. However, many social workers remain unaware of the rigors of this treatment regimen and the difficulties it presents. This article presents the results of a qualitative study of HIV-positive individuals who have struggled with the adherence issues endemic to antiretroviral treatment and seeks to give voice to their experiences. In the process the article also seeks to educate social workers about antiretroviral treatment for HIV, importance of adherence, and potential intervention strategies.

# (H)  Final Checklist

❑  Have you preserved the confidentiality of the research participants?

❑  Have you used gender-neutral language in your report?

❑  Have you properly cited work by other authors that you use in your report?

❑  Have you proofread your paper for grammar, punctuation, and spelling errors?

# RESEARCH PAPER OUTLINE

Title Page

Abstract

Introduction
     Significance and purpose of study
     Relevance to social work
     Research question

Literature Review
     Theories and concepts and variables
     Empirical studies
     Critical analysis and summary of literature

Methods
     Research design
     Data collection procedures
     Protections for research participants
     Measures

Sample
     Selection of sample
     Characteristics of sample members

Findings
     Visual presentation: Tables, graphs, and charts
     Narrative presentation

Discussion
     Your interpretation of findings
     Implications and recommendations for social work
     Strengths and limitations of the study
     Suggestions for future research

References

Appendices
     Consent form
     Research instrument

# WORKBOOK BIBLIOGRAPHY

American Psychological Association. (2001). *Publication manual of the American Psychological Association* (5th ed.). Washington, DC.

Berg, B. L. (2004). *Qualitative research methods for the social sciences* (5th ed.). Needham Heights, MA: Allyn & Bacon.

Bloom, M., Fischer, J., & Orme, J. G. (2003). *Evaluating practice: Guidelines for the accountable professional* (4th ed.). Needham Heights, MA: Allyn & Bacon.

Brophy, G. (2000). Social work treatment of sleep disturbance in a 5-year-old boy: A single-case evaluation. *Research on Social Work Practice, 10*(6), 749-760.

Dietz, T. J., Westerfelt, A., & Barton, T. R. (2004). Incorporating practice evaluation with the field practicum. *Journal of Baccalaureate Social Work, 9*(2), 78-90.

Fischer, J., & Corcoran, K. J. (1994). *Measures for clinical practice: Vol. 1. Couples, families, children* (2nd ed.). New York: Free Press.

Fischer, J., & Corcoran, K. J. (1994). *Measures for clinical practice: Vol. 2. Adults* (2nd ed.). New York: Free Press.

Epstein, I. (1987). Pedagogy of the perturbed: Teaching research to the reluctants. *Journal of Teaching in Social Work, 1*(1), 71-89.

Fineran, S., & Bennett, L. (1998). Teenage peer sexual harassment: Implications for social work practice in education. *Social Work 43*(1), 55-64.

Forte, J. A., & Mathews, C. (1994). Potential employers' views of the ideal undergraduate social work curriculum. *Journal of Social Work Education, 30*(2), 228-240.

Gabor, P. A., Unrau, Y. A., & Grinnell, R. M. (1998). *Evaluation and quality improvement in the human services* (2nd ed.). Needham Heights, MA: Allyn & Bacon.

Gibbs, L. E. (2003). *Evidence-based practice for the helping professions: A practical guide with integrated multimedia.* Pacific Grove, CA: Wadsworth.

Ginsberg, L. H. (2001). *Social work evaluation: Principles and methods.* Needham Heights, MA: Allyn & Bacon.

Green, R. G., Bretzin, A., Leininger, C., & Stauffer, R. (2001). Research learning attributes of graduate students in social work, psychology, and business. *Journal of Social Work Education, 37*(2), 333-341.

Green, S. B., & Salkind, N. J. (2005). *Using SPSS for Windows and Macintosh: Analyzing and understanding data* (4th ed.). New York: Prentice Hall.

Grinnell, R. M. (2000). *Social work research and evaluation: Quantitative and qualitative approaches* (6th ed.). Itasca, IL: F. E. Peacock.

Jordan, C., & Franklin, C. (2004). *Clinical assessment for social workers: Quantitative and qualitative methods* (2nd ed.). Chicago: Lyceum.

Kirk, S. A. (1990). Research utilization: The substruction of belief. In L. Videka-Sherman & W. J. Reid (Eds.), *Advances in Clinical Social Work Research.* Silver Spring, MD: National Association of Social Workers.

Kirk, S., & Fischer, J. (1976). Do social workers understand research? *Journal of Education for Social Work, 12,* 63-70.

Kjosness, J. Y., Barr, L. R., Rettman, S. (2004). *Research Navigator guide: The helping professions.* Boston: Allyn & Bacon.

Knight, C. (1993). A comparison of advanced standing and regular master's students' performance in the second-year field practicum: Field instructors' assessments. *Journal of Social Work Education, 29*(3), 309-317.

Leedy, P. D. (2001). *Practical research: Planning and design* (7th ed.). New York: Prentice Hall.

Lincoln, Y. S., & Guba, E. G. (1985). *Naturalistic inquiry.* Beverly Hills, CA: Sage.

Marino, R., Green, R., & Young, E. (1998). Beyond the scientist-practitioner model's failure to thrive: Social workers' participation in agency-based research activities. *Social Work Research, 22*(3), 188-192.

Marlow, C. (2005). *Research methods for generalist social work practice* (4th ed.). Pacific Grove, CA: Wadsworth.

Montcalm, D. & Royse, D. (2002). *Data analysis for social workers.* Needham Heights, MA: Allyn & Bacon.

Neuman, W. L. (2004). *Basics of social research: Quantitative and qualitative approaches.* Needham Heights, MA: Allyn & Bacon.

Padgett, D. K. (2004). *The qualitative research experience.* Pacific Grove, CA: Wadsworth.

Patton, M. Q. (1990). *Qualitative evaluation methods.* Newbury Park, CA: Sage.

Riessman, C. K. (1997). *Qualitative studies in social work research.* Newbury Park, CA: Sage.

Roberts, C., Piper, L., Denny, J., & Cuddeback, G. (1997). A support group intervention to facilitate young adults' adjustment to cancer. *Health and Social Work, 22,* 133-141.

Royse, D. (2004). *Research methods in social work* (4th ed.). Chicago, IL: Nelson-Hall.

Royse, D., Thyer, B. A., Padgett, D. K., & Logan, T. K. (2001). *Program evaluation: An introduction* (3rd ed.). Pacific Grove, CA: Wadsworth.

Rubin, A., & Babbie, E. (2005). *Research methods for social work* (5th ed.). Pacific Grove, CA: Wadsworth.

Siegel, D. H. (2003). Open adoption of infants: Adoptive parents' feelings seven years later. *Social Work 48*(3), 409-419.

Salahu-Din, S. (2003). *Social work research: An applied approach.* Needham Heights, MA: Allyn & Bacon.

United Way. (1996). *Measuring program outcomes: A practical approach.*

Weinbach, R. W. & Grinnell, R. M. (2004). Statistics for social workers (6th ed.). Needham Heights, MA: Allyn & Bacon.

Williams, M., Tutty, L. M., & Grinnell, R. M. (1995). *Research in social work: An introduction* (2nd ed.). Itasca, IL: F. E. Peacock.

Yegidis, B. L., Weinbach, R. W., & Morrison-Rodgriguez, B. (2002). *Research methods for social workers* (4th ed.). Englewood Cliffs, NJ: Prentice Hall.

York, R. O. (1998). *Conducting social work research: An experiential approach.* Needham Heights, MA: Allyn & Bacon.

# APPENDIX

| Stages of Conducting Your Research Project | One-Semester Timeline | Two-Semester Timeline | Completion Dates |
|---|---|---|---|
| 1. **Develop Your Research Question, Plan for Protection of Participants** *See Workbook Chapters 1, 2, 3, & 11* | 1 to 2 weeks | 4 weeks | _____ |
| 2. **Conduct Literature Review, Select Research Design, Determine Sample Design** *See Workbook Chapters 4, 5, & 10* | 2 to 3 weeks | 6 weeks | _____ |
| 3. **Develop Measurement Instruments** *See Workbook Chapter 6, 7, 8, or 9, depending on your method* | 2 weeks | 4 weeks | _____ |
| 4. **Pilot Measurement Instruments*** *See Workbook Chapter 6, 7, 8, or 9, depending on your method* | 1 week | 2 weeks | _____ |
| 5. **Collect Your Data** *See Workbook Chapter 6, 7, 8, or 9, depending on your method* | 4 weeks | 6 weeks | _____ |
| 6. **Analyze Your Data** *See Workbook Chapter 12, 13, or 14, depending on your method* | 2 weeks | 4 weeks | _____ |
| 7. **Prepare Final Research Report** *See Workbook Chapter 15* | 2 weeks | 4 weeks | _____ |

**Submit Final Research Report**          **Report Due:** _____

*\* Remember, you must have IRB approval even before piloting your instrument.*